ALL MOD CONS

How Much for a Little Screw?

Book 2

GRAHAM HIGSON

OLD BARSEY PRESS

First published in 2017

© Graham Higson 2017

Cover images © Graham Higson 2017

www.grahamhigson.com

All rights reserved. No part of this book may be reproduced, stored or introduced into a retrieval system, or transmitted in any form or by any means (electronic, mechanical, photocopying, recording or otherwise) without the prior permission of the author.

The moral rights of the author have been asserted.

Cat 00160217

ISBN: 978-1-5206310-5-9

*To the memory of
the MD's wife
1922 - 2015*

This book is a fictionalised memoir based on true events. Names, places and some of the timings have been changed.

THANKS

A big thank you goes to my beta readers:

Julie Haigh
A M Rothery

for their interest, time, professionalism, and comments for which I am grateful.

EXTRAS

For more information and features relating to the

How Much for a Little Screw?

books, please visit

www.grahamhigson.com

1

Tear Gas

MAGGIE NEWSPRINT DIDN'T LOOK pleased like she usually did when I went into her paper shop. I was carrying a bottle of butane gas on my shoulder – something that usually impressed her – and today she didn't even give me eye contact.

Now, I read somewhere that sub-consciously we can tell if someone is attracted to us because their eyes get bigger when they look at you. But if their eyes are naturally small, then significant eye contact can be hard to spot; and if they are large, then either they fancy you like mad or they've just got big eyes. You have to be careful not to misread the signs. Maggie's eyes usually opened up like saucers when she saw me. But not today. I should point out that I never encouraged her affection; she had her Steve, after all, and at that time my body was in wobbly negotiations with the Accountant.

Then I spotted why Maggie wasn't looking at me: her attention was clamped on a kid that was lurking over by the comics.

"Just take it through for me, Graham, love," she said, without looking away. I breathed a sigh of relief – okay, so I didn't really sigh exactly; it's just a saying, but you get my drift. "Sorry I can't come through with you, but –" and she raised her voice – "I'm watching the shop. There's a lot of thieving goes on and you can't be too careful."

"Yes, I know exactly what you want—"

"Stock doesn't come cheap and it doesn't come free, neither, does it?" She really was laying it on a bit thick. That kid would have to be deaf not to realise that she was on to him – whatever he was, or wasn't, doing.

"It's bloody expensive and I work damned hard to pay for it." My god, now she was even frightening me.

The lad was dressed in short trousers, blazer and nebbed school cap. Even for the mid-90s his school uniform seemed a couple of decades behind the times. So preoccupied was Maggie that she'd forgotten to mention that damned sticking-out shelf: it lurked below eye-line just right for collecting skin from my shins.

"Don't forget to mind your shins on that sodding shelf down there, Graham. I keep meaning to get it sorted." I spoke too soon.

Now, don't get me wrong, but while I never craved the attention from my grateful female customers (it's wasn't a sexist thing; I just didn't have any male fans), it was good to know that in Maggie's eyes I hadn't lost my appeal and that our gas sales were safe.

"I'm sorry I can't come in there with you, love, but –" and again she raised her voice – "I'm watching the shop. I've had lots of little thieving buggers in here, lately..."

At Little Sniffingham Hardware & DIY, we also got shoplifters, but generally our stuff wasn't so nickably desirable as it usually had the element of work associated with it. At least Maggie's retail surveillance meant that I could swap over the gas bottle in her heater and get out again without her piling into that tiny room and pressing her four-foot eleven frame against me in the claustrophobic confines.

Right, I was done and was just about to make a quick getaway when she grabbed my forearm and my feet made a Formula 1-style screech on her plastic floor tiles.

"Don't go yet, love. I might need some help," and she nodded towards the lad.

"Maggie, I really need to be getting back."

"Why? You can be my security guard."

I tried to reason with her. "Right this very minute, that lad's mates could be raiding *my* shop."

"At least you've got an apprentice to watch out for you."

"Yes, but he's a teenager."

"Oh yeah, forgot." She understood and her shoulders slumped, yet still she didn't take her eyes off the kid.

I thought another tack might work. "Where's your Steve?" – Whoops! As soon as I said his name, I regretted it.

She almost spat. "That mucky bugger of a boyfriend of mine is at work – at least that's where he's supposed to be." I never knew what she meant when she called him a "mucky bugger" and I didn't like to ask. Maybe he was rather keen, preoccupied or over-obsessed with intimate practices; maybe he chased after other women – ones less-demanding than Maggie; or maybe his personal habits were questionable. But seeing as Maggie was constantly trying to make our relationship much more personal, I rather suspected it was the last one.

She had turned to face me, taking her attention from the possible miscreant, and when she looked back she jumped – the spooky child had been magicked to the counter.

"Yes, what do you want?" It came out a bit sharp, I thought.

The boy handed her a wallet.

"And what do you expect me to do with that?" she asked him.

He pointed over to where he'd been eyeing-up the comics. "I found it on there."

That stumped her and she took the wallet from him, not certain what to say, the pair of them staring at each other. I was not an interested party and yet I was feeling distinctly uncomfortable. To break the awkward silence, I said:

"That's very good of you."

"No, it's not good of him at all!" Maggie's jab came quick as a flash. "Everyone's supposed to be honest. It's nothing special. He's done the right thing and that's all there is to it." She turned to the boy. "If nobody comes to collect this within the next hour, I'm handing it in to the police and they'll want your name and address—"

The kid's face went pale. He swallowed, just like Greville our apprentice did when he'd missed a sale or given out too much change. Maggie went on.

"If it's not claimed after so many weeks they'll let you have it, so come on, we'll start with your name."

"Can't I take a reward now? For being good?"

"We don't get rewarded for being good. We get bollocked for being bad, so come on, what do they call you?"

"I'll have that one," and he pointed to a medium-sized box of chocolates, the sort that gets sold for Mothers' Day, or for making up with disgruntled spouses.

"You bloody won't!" Maggie fired back at him. "You either give me your name or you can bugger off to school, where you're supposed to be."

He made a grab for a large block of chocolate from the counter display but Maggie's small hands clamped around his fingers like the jaws of an engineer's vice and he dropped it and scampered out, rubbing his reddened fingers, calling her every f—ing bitch under the sun. I felt she'd been a bit hard on him and was about to have stern words with her.

"So did I do right, Graham, eh? Come on, tell me, you know I value your opinion. What d'ya think?"

"Er, yes, I suppose that under the, er, circumstances..."

She backed away from me in a defiant stance. "I don't believe I'm hearing this – not from you, of all people!" she snapped. This was the first time she'd ever criticised me. The scowl on her face was an unfamiliar phenomenon, and then she twisted the knife (don't be alarmed; it's only a figure of speech): "That's just what Steve would say." She did a sort of sigh, looking as disappointed as I felt, and she opened the till to pay for the gas.

Heading towards the door, it felt as if I'd suffered a serious reprimand at school. It didn't feel right leaving her like this. I knew she was the sort to chunter away as awkward customers were leaving, but now she was dead quiet, and it didn't bode well. I stopped by the lottery display, remembering that I'd not bought a ticket that week, but something was urging me to turn back and try and make up with her. Suddenly I was pushed to one side as a tall man wearing a business suit and overcoat swept past to the counter.

Next I heard Maggie's voice. "Can you describe it to me? I hope you don't mind, but I've to be very careful with other folks's property."

Despite the man lowering his voice, I detected a tone of imposing authority and impatience. And I didn't like it. Turning, I couldn't see Maggie for his bulk, but her voice had changed and without even hearing the words I knew that I should go to her.

"It's not all here," he said, "It's quite a lot short, young lady."

Maggie's mouth fell open. "I never even looked inside it. I was going to hand it in to the police."

"Why didn't you?"

"To give you chance to come and claim it."

"That's exactly what I'm doing, but it's not all here, is it?"

"Honestly, I never touched your money."

"*Honestly?* You've no idea how many times I've heard thieves—"

"I'm not a thief—"

"You intended to keep this for yourself, so come

on, hand it over."

Maggie's mouth opened and, for once, no words came out. I did hear the sound of her swallowing. This wasn't the Maggie I knew.

"There's fifty pounds missing."

"Are you accusing me of ... pinching—?"

"Yes, I am."

"I don't have as much as that in the whole shop. You can search it, if you want."

"I think it would be better if we let the police do that, don't you? It would certainly save me the embarrassment."

Maggie didn't know how to take this, but I was certain that the vision of a pair of rubber gloves passed through her mind.

"Return my money and I'll walk out of that door and I'll say no more about this. You'll never see me again."

Maggie's eyes were locked on to his. "But I don't have it."

"Return my money this instant. If I report you to the police, you'll end up losing your business. No one wants to deal with a thief."

"But I don't have it! I haven't taken anyone's money. I don't steal..." These were like little chants as she opened the till, letting its drawer fully open so he would be able to see inside. There were two ten pound notes and three fivers, which – and this stunned me – she handed to him.

He reached over and – wait for it – lifted out the plastic tray to reveal the metal drawer beneath. There was nothing hidden there. I sensed desperation, but it didn't register with me, not until later.

Maggie went into the back room, emerging with her bag, from which she took seven pounds and fifty pence from her purse. Not a word was said, then she emptied out the charity box, counting out enough to make up the shortfall. Watching this strange display, I was tempted to believe that she had in fact relieved the wallet of fifty quid, and that this woman – fellow shopkeeper and friend – was indeed a wrong-un. It was true that I did not like this man, but right then – but only for a split-second – I felt myself disliking Maggie even more. The feeling of disappointment made my guts feel odd. The man screwed up the notes and coins in his hand and left, rather too quickly, when I came to think of it, with no further words of reprimand, nor even a mention of Crooks Anonymous. And then I noticed the stitching of his coat collar that was coming undone, and the tired state of his shoes, which didn't match the rest of him, being summery and for someone rather younger. Maggie looked away from me, her face beginning to contort. I could stay and try and make up with her, or leave her to her own devices, or see where the man went. A crowd of customers blocked the doorway and by the time I was out on the street, there was no sign of him.

2

Fools and Shoplifters

EVEN CARRYING A LARGE (empty) gas bottle, I could enter our shop without sounding the door bell – a handy technique preventing needlessly disturbing the others if they were working in the back.

"*We will exterminate!*" the mechanised voice belted out from aisle number 3, and I have to admit that it made me jump. Okay, it was a bit more serious than that because I actually froze – if only for a second or two, mind. I mean, what on earth was a real live Dalek doing on the premises? More to the point, what was a Dalek doing amongst the plumbing fittings? The answer came to me in a flush as soon as I pictured its fighting tackle, and I kept my head down, exercising a stealth approach.

Peeping from around the central heating gunge inhibitor, there was Greville, our apprentice, twirling from side to side, holding an erect, over-sized sink plunger in one hand and a drooping pipe-bending spring in the other. "*We will exterminate ... exterminate ... exter—*" He jumped a foot in the air when I tapped him on the shoulder. The look of embarrassment had to be seen; it was just priceless.

He went all out of breath. "Er ... it was the MD told me to clean—"

"You can get tablets for that," I said, wiggling

the limp pipe-bending spring. There was Greville's absent expression. "A Dalek's not much good with a floppy gun stick, is it? The voice is good, though."

"Eh, do you think so, like?"

"Yeah. You'll have to do it for Sharon and see if she can get you a part in *Doctor Who*?"

"What – you mean *really*?"

"No."

"Why not?"

"'They've stopped making it."

"I forgot."

The MD shuffled out of the office. "Who's stopped making what? I hope it's not one of our best sellers you're talking about."

"No, just *Doctor Who*." I expected to be launched into a silly conversation about *which* doctor, *what* doctor, the difficulty in getting an appointment with a doctor and the cost of prescriptions. Instead he surprised me.

"Oh, aye, that old thing. Well, the BBC's not daft. They'll get around to making some more of 'em, there's nowt no surer," and he went up the Key Hole and tut-tutted about the metal filings that hadn't been cleared from around the key cutting machines.

Greville moved out of earshot for when he was called to clean them. "So what happened, then – you know, with *her* at the paper shop?" And he winked. He had taken to keeping tabs on my promising, if non-existent, love life.

"You mean Maggie?"

"You look like she shagged you backwards into her rear space," and he laughed, then saw the

10

disapproving look on my face. "She didn't, did she? I mean, you look ... troubled."

"There's trouble, alright."

His face dropped. "She's not said owt, has she?"

"No?" He didn't know that I knew that he was secretly smoking, buying cigarettes from Maggie.

"Have you two fallen out, then?"

"Don't worry, Greville, it's just fools and shoplifters she doesn't tolerate – oh, and filthy boyfriends, whatever that entails."

The MD patted me on the shoulder. "By the way, we need to be keeping us wits about us. I was in yond friend o' yours this morning—"

"Maggie's?"

"No – her that can't cook or bake."

"Rita?"

"Aye, that's her, fancy accent, good as gold, grand lass."

"What were you doing in there?"

"I was having some breakfast – what are you looking at me like that for?"

"Nothing, it's just that you're still standing. Are you feeling okay?"

He gave me a playful smack on the back of my head. "Cheeky bugger, of course I'm still standing. It'll take more than a few rock hard bits of bread to kill me off."

"So what's she selling now?"

"Little pieces of dried bread, I ask you, and hard enough to sharpen your chisels on."

"Who on earth wants to eat dried bread?"

"It came with the soup."

"Soup – for breakfast?"

"No way was I having any of her eggs – she had her other customers picking bits of shell out from their fried tomatoes. Anyway, somebody tried to diddle her." He would have left it there, which was typical of him. But we wanted to know more.

Greville, unfamiliar with the term "diddle", thought it meant something different and fell about laughing. Even back then the youth of the day thought that they knew so much, so nothing changes there. We urged the MD to not keep us in suspense.

"A kid found a wallet under one of the tables – that was before I got there – and this tall bugger comes in – you should have seen him – and with this right superior, snotty way of talking to people. Anyway, he told yond lass the money was short – in the wallet, I mean."

"And said he'd call the police if she didn't pay him back?"

"Have you heard about it, too? Well, she was in a right state, poor lass. She's a victim if ever I saw one. Anyway, I got rid of him for her."

Greville had been taking all of this in, and looked at the MD with a mixture of disbelief and admiration. The MD went on:

"We-ell, it's an old con trick, with a new twist. I took one look at his shoes and told him that conning decent folk out of hard-earned money mustn't be a good choice if that's all he can afford to put on his feet. And he should go out and get an honest job. Then I told him to bugger off."

"You mean, just like that?"

"Aye, just like that," and he nodded, scratching

his ear.

"And what happened next?" I think that was me, though it might have been Greville.

"He left, and that was the end of it."

"Weren't you scared?" Greville's prayers about excitement in retailing had been answered, just so long as he could watch from a distance.

"Look, lad, there isn't a thieving bugger sly enough to catch me out," and, with an adoring wave to his admirers, he was about to return to the office to complete the monthly PAYE return (a tax thingy) when I stopped him.

"Something's just occurred to me. Maggie's been conned, Rita's almost been had with the same trick. This sort of thing was mentioned some time ago at the shop watch meeting – a con trick, here, a bit of sharp practice there, they start small, get bigger and bolder, and before we know where we are we'll all have been shafted right, left and centre. Then they go, move on to another part of the country, leaving behind a scene of town-centre devastation unparalleled since the Wall Street crash."

The MD looked at me, wondering if I was making it up. "No, that can't be right."

"Straight up," I told him, "it's a highly-organised gang. They did an area in Devon a year or two back, caused closures, redundancies, economic blight. They're probably still feeling it down there."

He still didn't believe me. "No, lad – him this morning, he were just a chancer, an opportunist, seeing how much he could get—"

"Yeah, fifty quid a time."

"People like that don't go round in gangs. They might have a mate—"

"An accomplice?"

"Well, aye, I suppose so—"

"And maybe another one somewhere, keeping lookout, perhaps?"

He couldn't discount it.

"That sounds like a gang to me."

3

Hard Words

"WHERE'S SHARON? SHE'S USUALLY here by now." I didn't think Greville was old enough to call her by her first name.

I'd set him the character-building task of sorting a mixed box of springs into order and see what he would come up with.

"She's having trouble with Gus, and, just so you know, it wouldn't be her place to help you with a piddling job like this. You should be done by now. What do you notice about springs?"

"They're sharp. Me fingers are done in."

"They'll toughen up. In broad terms, how many types of spring are there?"

"Who's Gus, when he's at home?"

I sighed. "Well, that's the trouble – apparently he's not."

"Is he her bloke?" He didn't like the thought that she might have loyalties elsewhere.

When Sharon did come in, she didn't look happy; her body language was not what I expected when everything was normal, whatever that meant, and I followed her upstairs to the staff room to tell her what had been going on that morning, and see if it would take her mind off Gus. She brightened when I told her the story of the MD tackling the conman and saving Rita fifty quid. When it came to Maggie she gave me the daggers look, making me glance behind in case she was taking exception to someone else. Then the pointing finger came out.

"You mean to say that you allowed that girl to get conned, without doing somefing abart it?" There was an unhealthy pause. "Lord, I don't believe I'm hearing this."

I tried explaining what had happened, but that only made things worse.

"So vis geezer tells her to pay up or she'll never work again—"

"That's when she handed over the cash."

"What – just like that?"

"Just like that, quiet as a mouse – well, chuntering under her breath, like she does, you know. But there's something else—"

"I should bleedin' well hope so. What I want to know is, what was you doing when she was being mugged?"

"It wasn't a mugging – she only gave him what he wanted—"

"And why would she do vat, eh? Go on, tell me."

"I need to tell you something else—"

"You didn't, no, tell me you didn't."

"I didn't what?"

"Tell me you didn't *believe* him…"

"Well, maybe for a split second, but …"

That was the thing about Sharon: she could read people like they was – I mean *were* – books. And I was no exception.

Her voice was even and steady: not a good sign. "You done vat girl a big disservice." It wasn't a question.

Turning away from me, she smoothed down her dress around her hips, like she did, adjusted her hair, straightened and grabbed her overall. She always looked smart, especially in that particular dress, and I'd never seen anyone else working in a shop who could look as fantastic wearing an overall. To me, Sharon was an icon amongst shop workers, but today I'd disappointed her, which was unusual. Hell – I'd disappointed Maggie, even before she was conned out of fifty quid. And, right then, I was feeling bloody disappointed in myself.

"This job ain't just about keeping shop – it's about keeping friends. And one day, Graham, when you need 'em, you may find you ain't got none left 'cos you've pissed 'em all off." And she went.

When I dragged myself downstairs, she had both Greville's and the MD's attention.

"... yeah, seen all this before, when I was working in the smoke. These baastards come wiv an arsenal of conniving and devious tricks. And we mustn't underestimate 'em 'cos they're good – so good you wouldn't believe. And brash. And unrelenting. And mean and confident. They don't take no prisoners. These scum will take from *anybody* an' they won't move on 'til they've conned *everybody*. I even seen 'em take coins from the homeless in shop doorways. Nothing and no-one is sacred."

The MD was nodding in agreement, which must have pained him; no one could have claimed that Sharon was one of his favourite people. So the old man believed *her*, but not me. Bloody marvellous. Greville looked frightened. She went on:

"We'll have to gear up, keep our eyes and ears open, look beyond what seems to be happening – what they want us to fink is 'appening. We gotta be two steps ahead – one step ain't enough. I seen businesses fail, livelihoods decimated, relationships ruined," and she looked at me. "I never believed this kind've filth would crawl as far north as this."

"So what can we do about it?" Greville was visibly shaking.

"You've been watching too many re-runs of *The Sweeney*," I told him.

Sharon's voice was piercing. "The boy's right to be wary. These people play dirty – cross 'em and they'll 'ave your 'ead off—"

Greville's eyes were like gobstoppers. "Really?"

Sharon pointed to him. "Foil 'em, but never, *ever* tackle 'em. You got that, Greville, my love?" She turned to the rest of us. "Vigilance, observation, knowledge. Keep this in mind – we're under attack."

We all made as if to get back to work, but she'd not finished. "And one laarst fing…" We waited for her dramatic pause, but really I think she was choosing the right words. "…the most important of all … we need to support each other – know what I mean, Graham? – or we'll all be going home with more than our bank balances in shreds."

I was going round the aisles with the order book when I heard Greville's lady customer raise her voice.

"That's what I've been told to get – decorator's cock. That's what it's called, so don't look at me like I'm stupid!"

Dropping the book, I shot to the counter so fast that I couldn't remember how I got there, but my chest was thumping, all the same – more from nervousness than physical exertion, you understand.

"Are you trying it on?" she said to him, her tone laced with menace.

I plonked a cartridge of caulk (a type of sealant) on the counter so hard it fell over, landing on her foot, which I accidentally touched as I picked it up – the sealant, that is. When I went on about its elastic properties and how long it should last, she bought it.

Greville looked as if he was in trouble. "But she asked for—"

"I heard what she said, but someone's been trying to make a fool of her, and when that happens it's up to people like you and me to prevent the customer's embarrassment. You got that?"

I thought I'd give him a few moments for today's lesson to sink in, but turning a corner I was accosted by Maggie Newsprint. Wrapping her blackened little fingers around my forearm, she dragged me up a short aisle with bypass flanges on one side and bolt croppers on the other, so you had to be careful where – and how – you stood. I was happy; she'd come to tell me everything was okay between us, so one thing less for me to worry about.

Her voice was lacking its usual friendly tone. "I want to get something very clear, Graham."

"You want to make *what* clear?"

"I'll pay it all back, you know I will." *What was she on about?* "Whatever else you think of me, my word must count for something, you've known me for long enough, surely. The charity box money – I'm talking about the charity box! I had to break in – I'd no other choice and that's all there is to it."

"But I don't understand why you gave in—"

"I didn't give in to nobody—"

"—when you didn't even have what that big bugger said you'd nicked."

"I felt like I didn't have any choice. One wrong word – that's all it takes – just one, and if the customers feel they can't trust you, well, you're as good as finished. It gets so it's all elbow nudges and funny looks, then it's no footfall and an empty till at the end of the day. But whatever anybody says about me, I will put it *all* back, every penny. Just so long as you understand." She seemed about to go, then turned back. "You were the last person I ever thought would…" and she looked away, straightened a tin on a shelf, then back to me. "So you'll put folk straight if they say owt wrong about me, won't you, Graham? Can I rely on you to do this one last thing for me?"

Of course she could rely on me – forever, if it came to it. Only something stopped me from telling her there and then, and I'd no idea why.

Looking so forlorn, with her short hair and urchin features, I just wanted to hug her – platonically, you understand, nothing ... you know. But I knew that our friendship was finished and it felt like a part of me had been ripped away. I wasn't used to feeling like that.

The MD wouldn't be pleased because for years Maggie had been most insistent on ordering gas bottles when the old ones weren't completely empty, even though I'd told her she was wasting her money getting them changed. So we'd been using them to heat our shop.

Maggie looked down, then back at me, tears of anger and frustration glistening on her cheeks. Wiping them with her fingers left grubby streaks of newsprint. Then she turned and left.

What did Sharon say about crime damaging relationships?

4

Sticky Problem

"AND HOW DO YOU fink you can tackle them baarstards all by yerself?"

I found myself clenching my fists in my overall pockets, and it occurred to me that I may look a bit like Greville did when he was bored, or he was thinking, so I took them out and flexed my fingers instead. Sharon was wiping down the draining board, which was one of the things she did when considering options.

"You're taking it bad about you and Maggie, aren't you?"

"I thought you'd approve of me feeling like shit about it."

She sighed. "And how's things wiv that accountant woman? She moved you into *her* place yet?"

Was Sharon trying to make me feel better? I had no idea. Maybe she was simply trying to confuse my feelings.

"I don't see what that has to do with any of this."

"You could always go see her, you know."

"I daren't do that until I can be certain she's not charging me by the hour."

"I'm talking 'bout Maggie!"

I shook my head. "I just so want these greedy, conniving, thieving buggers cleaned out of town."

"Making them someone else's problem, you mean?"

"You know that's not what I mean. If we could get them arrested, it would be a result. But we both know that they'd spend little time in prison, and before long they'd be back on the streets causing more untold damage."

"You can't very well plant yourself in every shop, waiting for these rogues to go in, can you? And if you could, you only know what one of them looks like. What about the others, his accomplices? Do we know how many there are? No, not a clue. Look, Graham, we don't know nothing about them. They could be anywhere. They rely on getting people's trust, which is why they don't go round wearing striped jumpers and Dick Turpin masks. I don't see what you can do, apart from be very careful, like everyone should be."

"Sharon, that's a great idea – I'll see if we can arrange an emergency meeting of the shop watch group. Yeah, spread the word, exchange notes, see what other cons have been going on, learn from each other – what's the word? Er ...thingy ..."

"Networking?"

"That's it. We'll do that and hopefully prevent any more damage."

"You might limit the damage, but prevent any of it? Nah."

"If I can help to prevent just one attack, it would be worth it. So let battle commence."

"It's bleedin' cold today," said Sharon, rubbing her arms.

Greville thought he'd put in his two-penn'orth. "If we kept the door shut, the cold wouldn't come in."

"Neither would the customers," I told him. "And cold doesn't come *in* – the heat goes *out*. Always remember your thermal dynamics."

"I don't wear them," said Sharon. "Bleedin' old-fashioned passion killers!"

"Well, I've checked the temperature," I called, in an effort to quell any rebellious mutterings, "and we are perfectly legal."

"You check it personally, did you?"

"The MD did."

"I should've known. He's probably fiddled the thermometer."

"It's these old buildings with cellars and stone floors. They had no conception of thermal insulation in the old days, and anyway, people were tougher – are you taking notice, Greville? That's a new word for you, *tough*."

He popped around the draught excluder stand. "What's a cellar?"

Sharon and I looked at each other. Was he serious?

"You know, a basement, a room under the

ground floor."

"What are they for?"

"This one was for storing coal." He seemed to accept this. "And meat." He made a sound at the thought. "It's okay, they kept them spotless."

"Wow! And there's one here?"

"The trapdoor's in the old bit, through there. Some years ago, when I was the apprentice, we used to have an old woman come in who liked to chat away to her invisible friend. The locals called her Daft Doris. Anyway, one day the council was ripping up the pavement and they broke our coal grate, leaving a hole in the ground. A few days later they got around to blocking it up and Doris came in, with her *friend*, who told her there was a cat in the cellar. I didn't believe them, but to shut her up I shifted all the stuff off the trapdoor and went down to look."

"Sounds like a right nutcase."

"I found a kitten."

"You never did! You're taking the p—"

I held up my finger to him and he stopped right there; he knew that dodgy language was not allowed, especially when the shop had a good reputation with its lady customers. We let Sharon get away with it; she instinctively knew if customers were about.

Rounding a corner, I discovered a teenage girl at the counter, with short dark hair, pointy noise and rather pretty. She was tapping her foot and looking annoyed. Teenagers did that to make themselves feel important. "Where's your Evo-Stik?" This wasn't an uncommon question with teenagers at that time, only this girl said it as a challenge.

"We've had to take it off the shelves." *And you know why that is,* I thought. Solvent abuse was a popular, and potentially lethal, pastime with some.

"Why's that? This shop's supposed to be self-service, isn't it? And don't think of telling me that you don't think I'm old enough, 'cos I am – eleven, seven, seventy-seven."

I took a deep breath. So far this hadn't been a good day. Yes, she was old enough to buy solvent adhesive – hell, I was only one year older than she was when I had a mortgage.

"What do you want it for?"

"Me dad wants it. He's doing up me mom's kitchen table. Got some nice Formica to stick on." It sounded reasonable.

"What size do you want?"

"A small tin."

"Right, so that's one two-fifty-mil tin of Evo-Stik Impact, there you go. You know to put it on both surfaces, let it dry, then bring—" I was just trying to be helpful.

She gave me a look of ridicule, paid for it, rather brusquely, said nothing more, shot me a scathing look and left.

"Don't you want a free spreader...?" I called after her.

I just caught a "Piss off!" as the door bell sounded.

5

Broken Eggshells and Brownies

RITA HADN'T BEEN ON the manor for long (as Sharon would put it) and I needed to check how she was and maybe educate her about the ways of the bad boys. The only problem was that our shop was busy that morning and there seemed an endless stream of people wanting tap washers (did you see what I did there?) – oh, and draught excluders. We sold loads of the stuff because plastic windows, with built-in draught seals, were still in their infancy and the majority of Little Sniffingham's windows were still made of wood, and rattled in unison during strong winds. Eventually, Sharon motioned for me to sneak out between coachloads of customers.

Despite what the MD had told us about what happened that morning, Rita didn't appear to be displaying any visible scars as she set down her plates of unrecognisable fayre.

"Hello, dear," she called above the heads of her grey-haired clientele. "I shall be with you presently."

I propped myself against the counter as there were no empty seats, which was somewhat unusual for Rita's café because, although her perfect, posh school intonation was something of a novelty for the locals, her cooking and baking was enough to strip out one's stomach lining. Then it occurred to me that, as it was bloody cold outside, the town-centre stragglers were actually using her café to park their backsides in the warm.

"You look rather ravished," she said, forcing a grin.

"I think that's famished."

"And I have just the thing for you – fried tomatoes."

It was tempting, but, remembering what the MD had said, I caught myself just in time. "No, it's okay, thanks, Rita."

"Oh, it's no trouble at all, and it would on the house, completely gratis for a dear friend."

"No, honestly, Rita, I couldn't possibly eat another thing," I said, doing all the motions, although anywhere else I could have killed for a bacon sandwich. "Oh, very well, then." She looked terribly disappointed – I mean ... *just* plain old disappointed.

I asked how she was feeling after the incident with the scammer that morning.

Somewhat shocked, she believed, hoping that it wouldn't completely manifest itself until she got home. Just before leaving I asked if she'd be okay. At a pinch, I could always assign Greville to looking after her for a couple of hours.

"Oh, I'll be fine, dear. Thank you, all the same. But will *you*, be fine? I do worry, you know."

"We'll be okay, thanks, Rita."

"No, I mean *you*, yourself. It's such a big shop you have."

"I can always call reinforcements. A few years ago, when I had a health problem, I rigged up an internal telephone system. We have five extensions, so help is only ever a phone call away." *Hmm, unless you're running the shop all alone,* I thought.

"Ah, so when I get my big coffee rooms and cake shop, I can come to you to wire up the internal communications, can I?"

"You know you can, Rita. I'll look forward to it. See you later."

Apart from checking on her, I hadn't achieved anything. It had been my intention to explain some of the ways that con merchants operated, but it occurred to me that I didn't know anything at all about con artists. Hell, I hadn't even seen through the one that had devastated Maggie Newsprint – the very same trick the MD had spotted. Once word got around about it, he would be the toast of the town centre, bestowed with countless Brownie points, whereas they'd be throwing rubbish at me in the streets.

Back at the shop, the rush now over, the four of us were huddled in the office, which wasn't the ideal place, especially when there were dishonest people around and we were, in effect, leavings tens of thousands of pounds' worth of stock unattended. But I remember there was a certain comfort being in there, together, somehow distanced from those who believe it is acceptable to steal from us.

Sharon chose her moment to make a point. "You apologised to Maggie, yet?"

That was when we heard the footstep. Greville donned a rabbit-in-the-headlights look. I think we all did.

"My god, there's someone out there!" I don't know why I whispered that; maybe from embarrassment if the customer were to hear me. I mean, it wasn't cool to leave your shop unattended.

"One of you had better get out and see to 'em," grumbled the MD.

Greville shot out of the door. I followed him, wondering why the door bell hadn't sounded. If someone else had worked out how to enter silently, then the stock was, literally, up for grabs. We searched the aisles and found no-one. Hell, the very sound of the footstep was so uncanny that we even looked in the understairs cupboard.

"Did *you* hear somebody?" Greville asked.

"Course I did. We all did."

We decided not to leave the shop floor unattended from then on.

I'd been in touch with Police Constable Skipper and suggested an emergency meeting of the Little Sniffingham Shop Watch Group, unofficially known as the No Nickers Meetings. With any luck it would take place in the staff canteen at Tesco's, where there'd be free tea, coffee and broken biscuits – something to look forward to. Yeah, I know we were a sad lot. However, that's not how it worked out.

Until now I had managed to avoid entering one particular shop in the town centre, with its expensive fittings and image that screamed "Expensive!" But, sitting on the tubular steel utility chairs that, so I'd been told, had been borrowed from the nearby municipal hall, I found the bright colours of the surrounding art work and paintings so much more refreshing to look at than displays of 5-lever deadlocks or toilet seats. Needless to say, Tesco had been unable to accommodate the Shop Watch Group meeting at such short notice, and so we were ensconced within the premises of Barrington King, the local art and picture framing shop – sorry, make that *gallery*.

I was one of the first to arrive, having gained admittance with great difficulty. The door-entry system, where you pressed a buzzer and waited to be let inside, seemed to shop-standard bog workers like me somewhat at odds with the traditional manner of allowing easy access to customers. Hmm, so by keeping the shop door open, maybe the MD and I had been doing it wrong all those years? No, I don't think so, either. Gilbert, the master framer, bespectacled and bow-tied, and still wearing his trademark woodwork apron, squinted down his long nose whilst considering if he wanted someone like me in his gallery.

"It's okay, I'm one of you," I said, fully aware that such a blatant claim would not convince him.

"Oh, I don't think so," he said, with a dry tone and whiff of superiority, reluctantly letting me in.

So there I was, sitting in the cheap seats in the most expensive shop in town, watching the other stragglers being admitted so much faster; there's just so much damned dust with hardware, you see, making other shop workers so much more acceptable. Gazing at the pictures, my vision began to wobble at one particular seaside scene, with the beach hut-lined promenade and the family playing ball in the sand. I could almost hear the sound of the surf ... a thousand miles away from the Little Sniffingham smut. I was awakened by someone sitting down heavily next to me, spreading out his knees like fire dogs. It was Roger, from the music shop.

"Eh, is it you that has that boat?"

I nodded. "I don't suppose you know anyone that wants one?"

He grunted. Of course he didn't; no one did.

"I've been after getting this meeting for ages," he said with a wink, nudging me to make a point. If I'd had the energy I would have been puzzled, but it had been a long and troubled day. "So at long last, some bugger's taken notice of me, he-he. And about bloody time."

"Glad to hear it."

"It's a real threat to our livelihoods – that's what the public don't realise – oh, no, not a bloody clue. They've no sense about what stuff goes on in large-town retailing, have they?"

"Er, which large town is that?"

He paused, turning to look at me. "Why, Little Sniffingham, of course. These wrong buggers have done an absolute stack of damage, millions of pounds' worth."

Why hadn't I been told about this? So Sharon was right – of course she was – in that the damage done by conning villains has far-reaching consequences. Roger was still going on:

"... destroying shops, making buildings unsafe, not to mention the huge clean-up operations. The glass breakage alone runs into millions, you know. Then there's your frontages – I mean, frontages aren't cheap."

I had to agree, even though we were so hard-up we'd made our own from wood, using hammered-effect paint to make it look like steel, which I was quite pleased with.

"Sometimes they've to get the army in to deal—"

"The army? For conmen?"

He paused again, twisting for a better look at my face, presumably to check if I was switched on. "You what? No, I'm talking about *con*-crete, not con-men."

Maybe I'd fallen asleep looking at the beach huts, so I had to ask. "What has concrete to do with this meeting?"

"I don't know why you're here," he said, with a hint of condescension, "but the rest of us are here to put our cases forward for concrete bollards, all along the pavements in front of the shops. As protection." He paused, testing my reaction.

"This is an emergency No Nickers meeting," I

told him, though I was conscious of keeping my voice lowered, in case I was wrong.

"You what? We have them once a month. No, no. In all my years trading in this town, I've never – *ever* – heard of an emergency one. No, mate, you've got it wrong somewhere. They just don't have 'em. Once a month, set in stone, my friend, set in stone."

"And why shouldn't there be some elasticity to a No Nickers meeting?"

He looked away, smirking. Maybe I was indeed in the wrong meeting – the very meeting that I had suggested to our local Crime Prevention Officer. Or maybe not.

"Well, I mean, *your* stock isn't as valuable as mine, nowhere near as valuable, I realise that, but the bastards could still ram a whopping big four-by-four into your frontage and bring the whole bloody building down, couldn't they?"

"Would they risk ruining a four-wheel-drive car—"

"They nick 'em! They don't use their own, talk sense. Don't you know that?"

Maybe my meeting suggestion had been gazumped, so I was tempted to stand and leave, but by this time I couldn't reach the way out because the seats were occupied with many familiar faces from the local shops. Some of them even brought members of staff with them; from Little Sniffingham DIY & Hardware, I had to go alone to get the latest on criminals and crime-stopping.

PC Skipper stood in front of a big, elaborately-framed painting of unrecognisable content, causing

Gilbert to fuss about easing him to one side so as not to obscure our view of it. He hadn't cottoned on to the fact that we were lowly shop workers and unlikely to ever be able to afford such over-priced tat.

"At approximately nine-fifteen Thursday morning," PC Skipper began, speaking like he was a witness for the prosecution, "an unidentified confidence trickster was successful in extracting the sum of fifty pounds from the owner of the newsagent's, one Margaret..."

When he gave me credit for suggesting the meeting, Roger groaned, uncrossing his legs, shaking his head and torn between leaving or sticking it out to save face. If he'd left right then he would have missed the police's confirmation that an organised gang of conmen and women had indeed moved into the area. Their true *modus operandi* would be to descend on the six town centres, leaving no shop – however small – untouched. We would need to be vigilant and suspicious of any deviation from the usual ways of taking payment suggested by the conmen who were posing as customers.

Brian from the sports shop spoke up. "What are we supposed to do if we get these criminals in our shop?"

"Under no circumstances should you tackle them physically," was PC Skipper's advice. "Anyway, it's unlikely that any of you will realise a confidence trick has taken place – until afterwards, when it's too late."

There were angry mutterings. Then a woman

called: "Can't you tell us what to look out for?" That suggestion was well-received. But I could guess the response.

"These individuals work in gangs—"

"So they're not exactly individuals then, are they?" For a reluctant attendee, Roger was getting into the mood.

PC Skipper was not to be thrown. "They work in groups, can quickly change appearance and it's not unknown for shops to be targetted by the same person more than once in a day, performing a different scam. They are more likely to attack when your shop is busy." I saw a few shoulders relax when he said that. "These scams encourage a feeling of trust, they will look you in the eye—"

"And rob us blind!" Just what I was thinking, Maureen, manager of Superdrug.

PC Skipper consulted some papers. "They have the whole valley, with its six towns to go at, so they're likely to move around the area within the day and spread their attacks."

"Ha! So by the time we've circulated a description on the ring-round system, it'll be well out of date, then?" said Maureen, one of the keener multiple managers.

We usually blasted such vital information through the ring-round system, each shop passing it on to the next on the list. The only problem was that not all shops had a spare member of staff to pick up the phone. *Blasting* around the shops was more sarcastic than descriptive.

"Police advice is, as ever, to exercise extreme caution. These offenders use a wide array of tricks, all sophisticated and psychological. An experienced scammer is plausible – victims have been surprised at just how easily they've been taken."

Usually, we left the No Nickers meetings with a feeling of empowerment, having heard about recent arrests and punishments meted out. But tonight we dragged ourselves out into the bitter cold air with unanimous cluelessness and despondency. So far, thanks to the MD, Maggie was the only victim, but the rest of us would open up the next day, with little other choice than wait to be picked off like glass windows by a gang of vandals. I wasn't looking forward to it.

6

Cash on the Counter

"WHOSE BED DID YOU get out if this morning?" asked Sharon when she arrived the next day.

"Mine. Why?" I wasn't in the mood for jesting.

"You've got a face like a slapped arse. But it's noffing to do wiv me."

"You're right, it's not."

She went off to another part of the shop – not to sulk; Sharon was beyond such infantile behaviour, but to leave me to my own devices and get over whatever it was that I was troubled with. But she soon found it necessary to tackle me about something else.

"Where's that boy? I need a stiff word wiv him. Oi – Greville! Get your arse here a minute." I heard him dragging his feet along the aisle towards her. He had an instinct about when he was in trouble. Right then I had other things to think about. "What you fink you're doing leaving cash out on the counter, eh? You been here long enough to know the MD'll have you out on the street for this – and that's after he's taken yer balls off."

Greville donned his blank stare, which was usual for him. She continued to bollock him and I joined them to find out exactly what had happened. He denied any knowledge of not putting cash away in the till, so if it wasn't down to one of us, then it must have been the MD himself what did it – I mean, *who* did it.

As if there wasn't enough for me to think about. "How many people do I have to watch out for? I mean, there's *him*—"

"It's me what watches out for the boy."

"I've not done owt wrong," he said, spiked with indignation.

"—our hapless apprentice—"

"Do I need a hat?" Greville turned to Sharon.

"—the shoplifters, the customers who don't know their backsides from a man-hole cover—"

"They're not all like that—"

"—the con-merchants, and now it looks like the MD is getting forgetful. I feel increasingly isolated, as if I'm losing allies—"

"Well, you've only yourself to blame for that, Graham." She took out her duster to throttle the life out of it.

I allowed her that little dig. Then something occurred to me.

"There's just one thing I think I should mention ... the MD's not arrived yet."

There were four young children, maybe five to seven years old, sitting on the pavement next to the door of the Abbey National Building Society (a long-established pretend bank and a national institution until some massive Spanish bank decided to take it over and shut down many of its branches; they wouldn't allow such an abomination to occur in Spain). Where was I? Oh, yes, these kids were on the ground, their legs sticking out in such a way that passing members of the public might trip over them. And they had begging bowls, making silly howling noises and saying they were starving. They'd already collected a few quid, and I watched from the doorway of Woolworth's further along the street until a woman came along and collected the cash from them, telling them to try harder, then drove off.

We didn't usually get beggars – genuine or otherwise – in Little Sniffingham, and it occurred to me if it might be more than a coincidence that these had turned up at the same time as the conmen. Then PC Skipper stopped by.

"Do you mind telling me why you're not at school?" They shook their heads. "Where are your parents?"

"We ain't got no parents. We're orphans."

"Even orphans need to be at school."

"We don't go to school."

"Well, in this town we send all children to school," and he got on his radio and called for assistance.

When I passed again ten minutes later, the confidence-trickster apprentices had gone.

Sharon had that sighing sort of look, guaranteed to make me feel like I'd been somewhere I shouldn't. "Where on earth've you bin? You ain't bin wiv 'er next door, 'ave you?"

She meant the travel agent's, where the adoring Gwendolin led a life of multiple issues with her equipment, which, fortunately, I was able to rectify.

"Why not? It was an emergency."

"It's always a bleedin' emergency wiv her."

"Straight up – she had some fluff in her RAM slot."

"I hope that's not one of them euphemism fings," she said, quick as a flash. I didn't know what she meant, but I sensed a quick change of subject was called for.

"Look, I've been thinking about our own problem – I mean the current one. We need some sort of back-up, don't we – for if we get one of these merchants trying it on in here?"

"It's not a question of *if*," she said, "but *when*. They're gonna turn up in here sure as Hell will freeze over if the Government scraps VAT."

"Talking of abbreviations, that's what I was coming to – what we need is CCTV."

Greville popped up from somewhere. "Don't you mean *acronym*?"

I fired him down. "No. It's an abbreviation. An

acronym spells a word." His head disappeared again. That piece of educational value would be forgotten by closing time.

"They don't come cheap, not even the piss-poor ones you see up and down the big stores."

"I didn't really think we'd be able to afford one. But if – I mean *when* – anything goes wrong, it would be handy if we were be able to play back everything that happened."

"And what about everywhere else, like where we get stock half-inched?"

I snapped: "I don't have time to think about shoplifters!" In the following silence, I sighed, almost letting down the image that I had everything in control. But Sharon knew me better than I realised.

"What's up, Graham? Or can I guess?"

I walked away, clenching my fists in my pockets, wondering if it were possible for me to slither us out of the mess. "Right now, at this moment in time, it's the con artists we need to concentrate on."

"Yeah, okay, I got that. But you shouldn't lose sight of everything else or you'll find you're blinkered when something else does poke you in the bum – like them baarstards at the bank. You gotta watch them."

"And the shoplifters, and the traffic wardens, and the VAT man." I closed my eyes, stretched out my fingers. The level of sewage was lapping at my chin – oh, don't get me wrong, I don't mean literally, it's just a saying, but one that reminds me just how bad it felt

"You still not taking any pay?"

Hmm, I didn't want Greville getting a whiff of that; it was bad for morale. "Where is he?" I whispered.

"The boy?"

"Can't do with him knowing—"

"How bad fings are, you mean? He's probably out back, listening to the butcher's girl. She was at it again, earlier—"

"What – in this weather?"

"How else can she generate some heat working in that fridge of a shop? They interrupted her, so she'll be wanting to finish it, whatever it was."

I nodded. "So at least the shop's secrets are safe, for now. Not so certain about the butcher's girl. Maybe I'm worrying too much. I mean, if we are stupid enough to allow these people to take our cash—"

"Hey, you be careful what you're saying about shop workers. They ain't stupid. You don't need to be stupid or half-baked to fall foul of these crims. They're clever, devious, deceitful and downright bleedin' dishonest, you mark my words. But they're also very clever. They assume that everyone else will treat them with respect and the fundamental assumption that they're as honest as we are."

"And we're sitting ducks for a gang of expert confidence tricksters whose sole intention is to relieve us of the cash—"

"Cash we need to fend off the bank wiv—"

"And the one tool that we could really do with as a means of recording them – for evidence, description and identification – we can't afford."

We stood there, waiting for the next customer, wondering if we were about to become the scammer's chosen mark.

7

CoDs Wallop

SHE WAS PRETTY, WHIFFING of perfume, smartly-dressed, not your typical suppliers' rep-come-delivery person. "Hi, are you the boss?" she said, placing a box on the counter.

"That depends," I said. I was always cautious.

"Well, if you are, I've got your package for you."

"I'm not expecting anything."

"Well, your boss is – from TCP Retail Solutions," and she pointed to the fancy printed label. The company was based on some industrial estate in Slough.

"What is it?"

"Sorry, I have no idea, I just deliver. When's the boss due in, then? I can call back later today."

"Not in until tomorrow."

"Oh, that's such a shame." I had no doubt that she meant it. "The thing is that I've driven here specially to deliver this to him—"

"What – all the way from Buckinghamshire?"

"Yeah, I know. They wouldn't normally send a driver with just one delivery, but it's an important order and the post can be so unreliable." Yeah, we all knew that. "Can you maybe get him on the phone? It's just that I need his permission to leave it with you, okay?"

"I'll take it and make certain he—"

"Sorry, but it's more than my job's worth to

leave it with someone else – unless I can get your boss's permission."

I couldn't think what the MD had ordered that was so special, and I have to admit that I was curious. Maybe it was a CCTV kit? I paused, then dialled the phone.

"Hi, it's me at the shop. There's someone here says you've ordered something and they need your permission to leave it ... No, I've idea what it is..."

The young woman called out that she'd like to speak with him, so I put her on.

"Hi, I have a parcel for you from TCP Retail Solutions. I'm meant to leave it with you personally, but if I have your permission I can leave it with your colleague in the shop ... ah, okay ... Oh, so you think it might be ... so yeah, it could very well be what you've been waiting for, yeah ... Okay ... It's ninety pounds payable on delivery, so how can we do this? ... Okay, so I can just tell him to take it from the till. Okay – sorry, sorry, I'm keeping you from ... So okay, yeah, you finish what you were doing and I'll get off ... okay, 'bye, then." She handed the phone back to me. "She says you've to give me ninety pounds cash on delivery from the till, and I'll also need your signature on my paperwork," and she produced a clipboard for me to sign.

I stared at her, only for two or three seconds, watching the confidence slither down a notch (it was the way she was standing). She bit her lip, glanced at the door, looked at the package, then forced eye contact again.

Sharon came out of the office, looked at me,

pointed to the delivery woman.

The woman put on her breezy voice. "Look, is everything okay? Your boss did say to pay me from the till."

"Is that my boss who sounds like she's just come off the set of *EastEnders*?"

"Yeah, she does. Why?" She laughed.

"She's standing right behind you – and really she's not my b—"

The young woman was out of the door faster than a chicken being chased by Ronald McDonald.

"Phew! That was quick thinking, Graham, ringing me in the office. And I didn't tell her noffing about paying cash on delivery. I'd already said goodbye to her, though through the door I could hear the little bitch still rabbiting on to me."

I didn't feel good, yet I should have been elated, having foiled an attempt.

"So how did you know she was bent?"

"I made a mistake, unintentionally – Slough is in Berkshire, not Buckinghamshire, but she didn't pick me up on it. And it wasn't just that ... little signs, big symbols, if you know how I mean. I have to give it to her – she was good, maybe too good, with her well-practised patter that kicked-in to foil anything I said."

"Good on yer, Graham. Come to think of it, some geezer phoned, day before yesterday, asking what days the boss was in so they could avoid a wasted journey. Didn't fink noffing of it."

We opened the parcel. Inside were two odd pairs of well-worn trainers.

"Blimey, I've heard footwear's going up in price,

47

but ninety quid is bleeding ridiculous. At least this is one up to us. We should be thankful," she said, touching my arm.

"Yes, but there'll be more battles. This is frightening, Sharon. Something so innocent-sounding, so plausible. They can throw anything they like at us and, most times, they'll get away with it. The town centre's gonna be like a war zone."

I could tell she had issues with my analogy, but decided to leave it. "I fink we better get the word round, hadn't we?"

"Yeah, but she's been rumbled. By now she'll be using a different disguise, using a different trick. I know I would, so any info we pass round now is already out of date. I just wonder exactly how many scams they've got in their arsenal."

Greville was clomping down the stairs and emerged with that silly grin on his face. "What was that about scams in arseholes?"

8

An Inspector Calls

I WAS OUT IN THE yard that we shared with the butcher's outside toilet and the off-meat container, which meant that in warm weather there were blow flies as big as Spitfires. When the butchers came out to use the bog, I would pause what I was doing and go inside, being the discreet person that I am.

I was marking out some plywood that a customer wanted me to cut, when this rather tall police officer came out to join me. His uniform appeared to have more bits and pieces adorning it than the usual, so I guessed that he must be someone considerably more important than the aforementioned usual. Hmm, so perhaps he'd come to talk about the scam gang? He came straight to the point.

"Would you mind explaining to me what your policy is regarding the sale of intoxicating substances to teenagers?"

"We ask them their age, and if we don't believe them, we don't let them have it. We've already taken Evo-Stik and such-like off the shelves so it has to be asked for over the counter."

He drew a deep breath. "You sold a tin of glue to a young girl last week."

"Short, dark hair, bit of an attitude? She wasn't young." He nodded. "She even told me her date of birth – eleven, seven, seventy-seven. And she looked it, so I sold it to her. I think she'd have beaten me up if I'd refused," I said, trying to lighten the mood.

"She was found the next morning in the early hours, with her head in a plastic carrier bag." My guts fell to the ground, or that's how it felt. "She later ran away from hospital and is currently missing. Her parents are devastated."

"Oh, my god. No doubt she'll be after more of it, then? Is that how it is?"

"So I'm not here for your sympathy. I want you to be very careful about who you sell it to. Is that understood?"

"Yes, yes—"

"Then I'm finished here – for now." He turned to go, then paused, maybe thinking he'd been a bit hard on me. "I'm just asking you to exercise care. If in doubt about what they might use it for, tell them you've sold out, whatever their age," and he was gone.

Greville rushed out. "What was all that about, then? Looks pretty serious when a copper with pips shoves his way behind the counter. Eh, you're not in bother, are you?"

"You know how we've not to sell solvent glues to minors—"

"Why can't miners have Evo-Stik?"

"What? Min-*ors*, not min-ers." I tapped him on the head. "Min-*ers* hew coal. Min-*ors* are people under twenty-one."

"I thought that was eighteen."

"You wouldn't trust eighteen-year-olds if you'd

been bollocked by the police like I just have. From now on, the minimum age for glue is thirty."

When we closed that evening, the MD opened a box containing a pile of hand-written envelopes. "This isn't the first time anyone's had a go at conning us," he said. "We've been getting these for years," and he handed round a selection of letters, each one addressed to us personally, and neatly handwritten, describing some deplorable situation abroad where someone was desperately trying to get family money out of a war-torn state, hampered by crooked government officials and ring-fencing bureaucracy. The tone was pitiful, yet with some attempt to regain dignity. "Every one of these is from Nigeria."

Greville picked one out and was soon transfixed. "Oh, this woman's father has died and they won't let her have his money... It's addressed to Graham. She says she prayed over it and selected your name because of its esteeming nature. That's nice."

"So what exactly is she wanting?"

Sharon gave him a clue. "Look beyond all the brown-nosing."

"Hang on ... her father was a wealthy dealer ... She wants your honest co-operation and confidentiality to be reunited with her father's wealth so she can look after her cousin and seven children who have…"

I gently took it from him. "There's a box full of them, all personal, all hand-written, all heart-breaking tales, so very desperate. I remember the first one I ever opened. It seemed so easy to help – but what made me think twice was that it seemed *too* easy, and I'm naturally suspicious—"

"Not with that baarstard that screwed Maggie, you wasn't," said Sharon.

"—yet I was torn by the personal touch of the hand-written letter."

Greville wasn't letting it go. "Hang on … that one said the money could be transferred to a British bank account and all she wanted was some account details … she was offering *two million* US dollars – wow! I mean, all that just to get her own money out of the country." He was almost drooling over the possibility and picked up another one.

"No, don't look at any more, Greville, my love." Sharon touched his arm. "These are not nice people. They're crooks, every one of them, and they'll take your money—"

"No! That woman was wanting to put it in my account—"

"You mean my account, Greville."

"Whatever, but you'd have paid her what she wanted and you'd keep the two million. Easy money."

"Too easy. It would have ended up with me being asked to pay the transfer fees up front, then it would all have gone quiet, after I'd given away a few hundred quid – or more – to these people."

"Yeah, not to mention doing bird for his trouble."

Greville looked troubled and indignant; not a good combination. "Bird? Like pigeons?"

Sharon gave him a playful tap on the head. "No – bird lime, *time*!"

"What's bird lime?" he said, looking at me.

"Prison!" I said. The thought horrified me; one word was enough.

"So none of this is, well, *real*...?"

"Going down the hammer'd be real enough."

"Hammer?"

"Hammer and nail – *gaol*." That's not official rhyming slang, by the way: she was playing with him, trying to lighten the mood. After all, the lad looked devastated, his faith in human nature just about wiped.

"Better make him some coffee," said the MD. "He'll need his senses perking up for what's to come." What was that, exactly? We looked at him. "I'm talking about the onslaught. Things are about to get mucky."

9

Cam-pain

GREVILLE WAS GUARDING a large cardboard box on the counter.

"Er, I hope you didn't pay for that cash on delivery to some young woman with a nice bottom." I was joking, and thought he'd fall for it, but instead he lifted the lid, trying, without success, not to smile. Inside were three units, all made by Canon ... and one of them was a video camera.

"I got me dad to lend you this," he said. "It cost him a fortune when we were kids. He wanted to record us all growing up."

"You mean … there are more at home like you? " I asked, feigning fright.

The camera wasn't exactly small, nor was it the ginormous size one expects from ex-Soviets, but neither did it take small tapes – in fact, the full-size tapes didn't even go in the camera, but in a separate video cassette recorder. The third unit was the power pack.

"What do you think? Can you use it? Will it come in handy?"

"It certainly will, Greville. The picture quality is going to be superb. Only thing is," and I looked at him and the MD, "where are we going to put the camera? I mean, it's not small and lightweight, is it?"

The boy was perplexed. "You mean it's too big?"

The MD stepped in, reaching out to handle it, almost spraining his wrist. "Nay, it'll be fine. All it needs is some neat little bracket making to fasten it to the ceiling. It'll record everything and be a big deterrent to the bad buggers, when they see it. Aye, it'll be right. And maybe make a shelf just round there, out of sight, to take the recorder and this 'ere power thingy. There's a socket round there that it'll plug into."

"So, that's sorted then. Well, thank you, Greville, for making this available to us. Once the MD gets it all set up—"

"Eh, I said nowt about setting it up."

"You did. You've got it all planned out, making a bracket, where to plug it in..."

"I didn't say I was gonna do all that. I was giving you lot the benefit of my advice. So get on with it. I'll be in the office if you want to ask me anything."

Making a bracket for what is essentially a shoulder-hugging television camera was not easy. In fact, it was made from over sixteen pieces of steel Meccano-style corner braces (right-angle steel with bolt holes), lovingly fastened together with brass machine screws, washers and nuts – lots of them. We fastened it up to the ceiling, allowing it to swivel using a nylon cord with a couple of lawnmower handle grips at the ends. In #1 position it would look down at the till area, and, swung around to position #2, it would cast a wider sweep of the shop. Okay, don't laugh: the arrangement did look a little Heath Robinson, but it worked, and whenever I meet up these days with the old staff we still laugh about it. I only wish I'd taken a photograph; the bracketing might have looked a joke, but the camera itself looked a damned serious piece of kit. Oh, and the television we used was an old black and white portable from the MD's caravan, so at last we were set up and ready for battle, this time with some ordnance behind our lines.

The MD squinted up at it and nodded his approval. "Do you think you've used enough nuts and bolts there, lad?" he asked.

"Now we've got the means for identification and education," I said, with some pride, "a major tool in our plan of campaign."

Greville popped up from round a corner. "What was that about a can of champagne?"

I was late at the shop the next day because a woman had wanted me to give her a quote for waxing her chest. She was a little put out when I told her I refused to work with silicone, that only fine beeswax made from a traditional recipe would do, particularly for such a fine, antique example as hers. Actually, had she insisted on me using the modern crap with space-age chemicals, I might just have given in; we needed the money, simple as that.

Greville looked like someone had just smacked his face: it was red, his mouth was drooping further than normal, and Sharon had her arm around his shoulders. I asked what was up. A man had bought a packet of picture hooks – one of the cheapest items we sold – and paid with a ten pound note. At first I thought they were about to tell me it was a forgery, but no.

"Greville gave him his change, counting it out into his hand like we've trained 'im. Then he says he paid with a twenty."

This was an old trick, which was why we had fitted a clip (home-made from a piece of aluminium venetian blind) to the till, in which we placed notes until *after* the change had been given out, and only then was the note supposed to be placed in the drawer. So what had gone wrong?

Sharon prompted him to state his case. "His tenner was in the clip. I counted out his change in his hand. But there was a queue—"

"So you banged the tenner in the drawer and closed the till—"

"And that's when he said, 'It was a twenty pound note I give yer'. I knew he hadn't, but he stood just there, never shifted, didn't bat an eyelid, and all the other customers went quiet. They were all staring at me."

I looked at Sharon. "The intimidation technique."

"I mean ... it – it *could* have been my mistake, I could have got it wrong..."

Sharon squeezed his shoulders. "So I got the old

man out to do some serving an' the boy and me balanced the till, just to check. Ten quid short."

"What about the video?" Hopefully, I looked up at the camera.

"The bleedin' tape ran out."

"Great! We have the best camera in town and the tape runs out! Bloody marvellous!" So we were back to the non-technologicals. "What did he look like?"

Greville tried to be helpful. "Five-eleven, beer gut, glasses, beard, black and white speckly jumper."

"It's a disguise. They'll know that we have a ring-round system and the best way of foiling it is to look pretty damned individual." I looked at the apprentice. "Close your mouth, Greville. By now he'll be a gorgeous blonde with high heels, swinging her hips along the high street."

"What, really?" he asked, his mouth agape again.

"No. Look, don't worry about it. It's only a tenner and, unlike some of the big shops, you won't have to pay it back."

Sharon let him go. "It could have been much worse."

"Yes, but think how bad it would be if we lost ten pounds every day – the bank will foreclose on us if I don't pay the full amount on time. That ten pounds could literally be the difference between rolling and dole-ing."

"I once played a conman's girlfriend – well, I was his prostitute—" Greville made a strange noise; that should teach him to listen in "—who he'd rescued from a man what squeezed grease for Bulgarian tractor bearings. No, I didn't understand it, neither, and I don't fink the audience got it. We shut down after three nights, so it was back on the dole for me – which is what some of this lot round here can look forward to if we don't put a stop to these scammers."

"You're right, we've got to catch at least one of them," and I shot out the door, making it the fastest trip through the town centre I'd ever done, calling in every shop, having a rapid scout around, ignoring the comments and greetings from the staff. Yeah, I know what I'd said about him changing his disguise, but it was worth a shot, just in case. If I could just get one of the gang, the police would surely get him to reveal the others.

And all of that running did get the blood pumping around my body, which is always a good thing. I slept better that night. But the bad dream was still there the next morning.

10

Bank Job

RAM-RAID ROGER'S SHOP was a modern, aluminium-fronted emporium just along the street from us. Inside it was like ours, with almost every square inch of wall space covered with stock. There were purpose-made racks housing guitars, violins and keyboards, and a separate sheet music department that was big enough to be a shop in its own right. Compared with our displays – mostly home-made from plain timber – his were illuminated, branded, high-spec units made from polished ash and chrome, and when the sun bounced off the Post Office glass across the street you could be dazzled as soon as you walked in.

"Now then, Graham," he began, all friendly, which I thought was a joke, seeing as how at the No Nickers meeting he'd not been able to stand the sight of me. He was standing by the Roland display, with his arms folded, all business-like, "How do we tackle this set of bandits that's determined to mug us for every last ha'penny? I take it you know we've been done, don't you?"

Just then, I spotted the MD was looking through the sheet music, probably searching for yet another book of Jim Reeves numbers. Or Val Doonican.

Roger went on. "We may've been lucky. The bank says we could get compensation, but I want you to know that this trick wouldn't have got past me. I'd have spotted it a mile off."

All I'd heard was that he'd lost all his Saturday takings, so how did it happen?

"They'd stuck a notice on the night safe." He must have seen my clueless expression. "At the bank – the overnight night safe! You know what I mean, surely."

Yeah, I'd forgotten about such expensive luxuries. It had been years since we could last afford to use that service. Sticking your cash in a special wallet and depositing it in a securely-locked drawer in the bank wall was an old and trusted means of keeping it safe until the bank next opened and paid it into your account – so what had gone wrong?

"Well, this notice said the night safe was out of order so customers had to use the normal letter box in the bank's door – yes, I can guess what you're thinking. You wouldn't have fallen for that, neither, unlike..." and he motioned behind him to the young woman with red – and I mean dyed, vivid red – hair who was working at the counter. She lifted her gaze slightly, as if she knew she was the subject of some derisive comment from her boss. "...dopey lass."

"She must be feeling pretty bad about it. What exactly did the notice say?"

"Oh, it had the proper logo on it and everything, looked all very official."

"Oh, so you saw it yourself, then?"

He hesitated. "Well, I'd driven her round there, doing the lass a favour."

"But it was *your* money—"

He closed his eyes, shifting his weight from one foot to the other. I thought I'd better change tack.

"I take it the con artists had shoved a net through the letter box, so they could retrieve it all later when the street was quiet."

"Yes, exactly. It's the first time it's ever happened in this town, so the manager's ... you know. But what I want to know is what we're all going to do about it? I mean, we're sitting here like lemons—"

"Lemmings—"

"—waiting to be picked off. We need a plan. What do you suggest?"

"Me? I don't have a clue, apart from what was said at the meeting."

Just then, the MD sidled up, with his new Jim Reeves song book in a crisp paper bag. "Just remember this – these conning buggers are bloody sharp, and to foil them we've to be sharp as shit-house rats."

We heard the footstep again, in the very same place outside the office door. I went out to find no one there, so I asked Greville, but he'd not seen anyone.

"Maybe we've got a ghost," said the MD. He was joking, but at that time, particularly when we were being menaced by a certain section of the living, the possibility of being haunted by the dead didn't seem an unreasonable theory.

I was considering this when Maggie's Steve came in. He looked fit to kill someone and at first I thought it was me.

"I've come to tell you Maggie's shut down, closed," he said.

I looked at my watch: it was a quarter to four, and she'd surely miss the kids-going-home-from-school trade. Maybe she was ill ... but why send Steve to tell me?

"She's shut for good." He still had the menacing look. "She's been with t' police all morning." I didn't know what to make of this, but there was an atmosphere of foreboding. "They're charging her with passing out counter-forged notes."

"You mean *counterfeit*—"

"Yeah."

"Forgeries – Maggie?"

"In people's change."

"And has she really been doing that?" *What a stupid question!*

"Oh, yeah," and he turned and went, calling as he reached the door, "And she won't be wanting no more gas from you."

I looked around for Sharon, expecting her, for some reason, to be standing right behind me. But I was alone. She would have only rubbed in my despicable treatment of Maggie, and she'd have been right. If only I'd put my brain in gear when the big bloke was going on about his wallet, I would have spotted the glaring errors and asked

Maggie if she had actually seen him in her shop that morning, when he claimed he'd left his wallet behind. Simple! The layout of her shop was long and straight; she missed nothing, yet so critical was her financial position that, when tackled by an experienced scammer, she buckled whilst I stood on and watched ... and allowed it to happen. Somehow, the predicament she was in right now seemed to be a natural progression that was all down to me.

PC Skipper sent round a recorded message about local homeowners being conned into paying cash-on-delivery for packages that contained only old books and telephone directories to add a bit of weight and perceived value. In just one morning the scammers got away with over £500 by knocking on doors in just one tiny area. How much would they net spending another few weeks in the valley? This trick seemed to be from the same page as the CoD parcel scam that had been attempted with us. The advice for shops was not to accept any delivery until they were absolutely certain about the contents.

Some of the multiple shops' staff took it a little further when they found to their cost that their employers refused to cover any losses. The staff retaliated by refusing outright to accept any delivery – not even their usual stock drops. We were all trading in the same town centre, yet there seemed to be two separate and distinct worlds where multiple and independent shops were concerned. At that time I felt thankful that I didn't work for a large company.

The day after, reports came flooding in about staff being mislead when customers asked them to change high-value bank notes for smaller currency. The reason for wanting change, so they said, was to feed the parking machines. And they got away with it, even though at the time all the car parks were free. It was only when trying to balance the tills at the end of the day's trading that the shortages showed up in just over 80 shops, netting the scammers over £800. It appeared to be a confusion tactic, but no one could remember just how it worked. Fortunately, we'd been spared that one, which I put down to having foiled the CoD parcel scam. It looked like the scammers were being wary of our shop.

Descriptions of the scammers reported by the other shops were vague, potentially applicable to 95% of the public. The shops with CCTV had provided stills of their culprits, but every one was in black and white, grainy, fuzzy and blurred.

I was desperate to build a profile of the tricks and the tricksters – how they looked, what they did, how many different members there were in the gang. Did they belong to one family? Had they maybe been in prison together, and met and exchanged tricks? The answer was anyone's guess.

Sharon and I were talking about Maggie.

"The poor girl's a bit beyond the stage where a kind word could help, ain't she?" I asked if that was another dig at me. "I can't believe she'd do such a thing. I never realised just how desperate she was."

"Of course she didn't do it! At least not intentionally. Now you're the one who's doubting her integrity."

"I don't mean to. It's just that we don't know noffing abart what's going on, now, do we? I don't fink I can stand this."

"When you think about it, I suppose anyone's capable of making a mistake, particularly in this day and age, when everyone's in a hurry to pay up and get out the shop as fast as possible – which is why I'm going to call and see PC Skipper on my way home."

"He'll have gone home himself by then."

"I know, that's where I'm hoping to find him."

11

Hot Fuzz

I KNEW WHERE HE lived because, when I was the apprentice, I'd gone with the MD to deliver a load of hardboard door panels to this house, and the woman there had been telling us about her son who'd just joined the police force. I'd remembered her surname and, together with PC Skipper once mentioning at a meeting that he now lived in the parents' house, I didn't need any further clues. A good memory can certainly come in handy.

He was surprised to see me, yet invited me straight in. I felt that a little social chat might be in order before I got down to the business of demanding the keys to Maggie's prison cell.

"Ah, I see you've removed all the hardboard flushings on the doors." To explain, when in the 60s and 70s people covered the old panelled doors with sheets of plain hardboard, we used to say that they had been flushed; nothing to do with toilets, so nothing to be concerned about. That's what we'd been delivering, all those years before.

"Yes, but my dad never liked them plain, which was too late once he'd nailed them on, so when he and my mother moved out I thought I'd take them back to how they're supposed to be."

I was instinctively drawn to running my fingers over the panel beadings, admiring the care with which the old 1930s' paint had recently been removed. Sometimes you have to admire people's patience.

"Good stuff, that Nitro-thingy, isn't it? My wife bought it from you."

So, maybe a little more small talk wouldn't go amiss before getting down to the nitty gritty.

"Talking of doors, why has Maggie Newsprint been locked up?" Ah, mouth and brain not in mesh.

That had him! "Maggie who?"

"Maggie – I don't know her surname – the newsagent on the high street." To be honest, to this day I still don't know her surname.

He took a deep breath. "Ah. As far as I know, she was held for questioning—"

"She's a young woman with dependents."

"So why weren't the police made aware of this, I wonder?"

"She's certainly no criminal and I demand—"

"So she has children?"

"Well, one."

"We weren't aware of this. Boy or girl?"

"Boy. Steve."

"I didn't know. Well, I can put your mind at rest. She's not in custody now. They've finished with her, so far as I know. They'd have only held her until all the statements had been collected."

"Surely, you don't believe that she'd knowingly give out dud notes? I mean, doesn't the law allow for accidents? I don't know how else I can say this – everything's going mad."

I was marching around PC Skipper's kitchen, and it felt like some form of drowning. I remember it well. He asked me to sit down and calm down –

in fact, it might not have been a request. Then he got out some of the forgeries.

"Take a look at some of them. I borrowed these to take them around the shops tomorrow, so that the staff can see what they look like, how they feel between the fingers, because that's the best way of telling if a note is real or not. The words Bank of England are supposed to be raised."

He took the notes out of a plastic bag and laid them in front of me. Each one had been desecrated with wording by various enthusiastic police officers, each one determined to display the standard of their education. Some notes had been labelled more than once, presumably in case there was any doubt –

COUNTERFEET   FORJED

DUDD   COUNTERFITE

"And all of these came from Maggie's shop?"
"Only one of them did."
"*Only one?* So why was she frog-marched out in the street and shovelled into a police car? Now she's closed her shop for good. People won't feel she can be trusted. Where will the Little Sniffinghams buy their lottery tickets? Where will they buy the sad excuse for a local newspaper? Where are the intellectual think-tankers supposed to buy their copies of *The Sun*?"

"It was a member of the public reported her. The police had no other choice than to act."

"Are they pressing charges?" He didn't answer,

so I took that as a yes. "And has any of your lot considered that this fine, morally-upstanding member of the public might just have been given this note in another shop?"

I stared at the notes, then picked them up to rub between my fingers. I have to say they were good, not even feeling like they were printed on ordinary paper. I think we, too, could have been passing examples like these – unwittingly, of course. I asked which one Maggie had given out. He pointed to one of the twenty pound notes. An idea tumbled into my mind – actually, it felt like an avalanche, and a bloody great big one at that. I would need to choose my next words with care.

"Did your people—" PC Skipper liked to talk about his colleagues in the third person, but he was, after all, one of them, "—check Maggie's till in case she had more forgeries?"

He sighed, thinking about it. "I feel they would have done," he said. "It would be standard practice in those circumstances."

"Well, I certainly would, and I'm not a crime expert – apart from being brought up watching *Colombo*, *Juliet Bravo* and *Inspector Morse*." I paused for effect. "So did they find a fifty pound note in the till?"

Now it was his turn to think. "I'm unable to confirm that."

"Do you see what I'm getting at? Why would Maggie give out a twenty in change – dud or otherwise – if the customer hadn't given her a fifty? And that is unlikely because for the past year or so you've been advising local shops not to accept fifty pound notes because loads of them are fakes."

"So if there wasn't a fifty—"

"Then the customer was given the fake twenty somewhere else – and probably from the bank, because I was done there, not so long ago, by one of the cashiers, would you believe?"

I got up to leave, having given him enough to think about. "We have a big problem out there, with the scammer gang. They're the ones you should be arresting, not people like Maggie."

"Serious manpower shortages—"

"And how long, exactly, did it take your colleagues to get a cop car and enough officers to round up the highly-dangerous Maggie, public enemy number one? I'll bet you weren't shuffling from one foot to the other, wondering about cancelling holiday leave just to bring in a defenceless and totally-innocent and unoffensive woman." Maybe calling Maggie *unoffensive* was a bit strong, but I let it go.

He nodded. "If it had been down to me … but I'm just the CPO."

"Even so, I notice that you rounded up those kids begging outside the Abbey National. Where did they come from? You're bound to have their addresses, and, more importantly, the addresses of their scamming parents."

"I don't follow."

"They were apprentice scammers, every one of them."

"No, they weren't. They were here with their parents, visiting a sick relative. Nothing to do with the gang, nothing at all."

Oh. Hmm. Right then. I got up to leave, then he held up his hand.

"How's your list coming along?"

How did he know about that?

"It's not. I have half a dozen cons and only two descriptions of the baddies."

"Now if any of the shops could get at least one of these rogues on video, that could give us something to work with."

"Despite the disguises?"

"There's not a lot they can do with their faces, not without looking like clowns or children's entertainers. It's when they change their hair and clothes that people get confused. So a face would be helpful."

I told him that we now had CCTV, and that every day we were hearing tales of shop staff being fleeced, losses that some staff were being made to pay themselves. "And what's worse is that because they feel so bad that they've allowed themselves to be conned, not only do they make up the loss, they're also ashamed to report it. Those buggers are causing hardship and misery."

He considered this for a moment.

"What would you say if, let's say, certain information was to come your way that should help both you and the other shops? I shall only say this once, that none of this is official, nor can it ever be mentioned."

"What kind of—"

"You'll have to wait and see what happens. Maybe you'll just happen to find something and decide to open it to see who it belongs to, if you get my drift." I nodded. "Right. Now, television is one thing, but you know what all the shops could really do with, don't you?"

"Besides a cop on call in every one of them?"

"Instant communications, switched on all the time so everyone can be alerted without having to break off serving and answer the phone. The criminals'd enter, weighing up what they think they can get away with. Then they'd hear the radio chattering away in the background and they'd be off double-quick to try their con tricks in pastures new. How does that sound to you?"

I saw the possibilities. "Sounds to me like a double-edged weapon – the warning messages get passed round simultaneously, and the sound of the radio messages acts as a deterrent."

He motioned with his hands that we were operating on the same wavelength. "That's certainly what you need. If only we knew whatever happened to the old police walkie-talkies."

I don't know why, but I almost expected him to tell me not to be surprised if I just happened to trip over a skip full of them in the street. He must have read my mind. "No, no, you'll have to organise them yourselves. But it's an idea, don't you think? The word is that these individuals have a lot more to offer in the way of tricks, so my advice would be to get yourselves fixed up and on air as soon as you can. The ring-round system does have its limitations. So is that everything?"

"Could you do one more thing for me?"

"Well, if I can…"

"I have something I need to say to Maggie, but I

need her address."

He shook his head, leaving me in no doubt that I wouldn't get it from him.

12

Roger Roger

"NOW THEN, GRAHAM, HOW are you?" Ram-Raid Roger was looking, and sounding, pretty pleased with himself. He didn't see his sales girl go "tut" and shake her head. I wondered why I had been summoned. "I've called you in—" Ha! He's called me in like some low-at-heel employee, "—to have a word with you about the current crisis that we are each of us facing. I think you'll agree that this is a step-up from merely getting the odd reed or tuning fork nicked, isn't it? The young girl on the checkout in Woolworth's was done with a simple note exchange – yesterday, I think it was."

"That's a common one, an old favourite." I sounded like an expert, which frightened me because I was as green as the next man.

"Ah, but just listen – it was a forged note that he got her to take. That was the con."

"I'll need to make a note of that."

"Are you trying to be funny? These are young, inexperienced people – our nation's future – that are being stripped of their cash and their dignity."

He should have seen the facial expressions from the red-haired girl.

"My pun was unintended," I said.

"And I should think so."

"Look, Ram – er, Roger – why am I here?"

"That's what I was coming to. A little bird—"

Oh, please spare me, "—has told me that you are wanting to kit out the whole town with..." and he looked around cautiously, lowering his voice, "radios." He straightened.

"It's not a secret. And I can't see that happening. They're too expensive."

"Ah, well, that's where you are mistaken, my friend. Come with me."

And he led me through the back and up a spiral staircase to the upstairs rooms. I'd had no idea just how much space he had – well, I call it space, but actually it was stuffed with boxes printed with names such as Shure, Yamaha, Roland, Boosey & Hawkes. I was a little impressed, I must admit. We squeezed into one room that had cardboard boxes on shelves and sticking out into the aisle. He tapped one of them.

"Job sorted. What do you think these are?"

"Radios?"

"Correct."

"How many?"

"Eighty-seven."

There were just over one hundred and twenty-five shops, but I was aware that not all of them would be interested, mainly because of the price.

"How much?" I didn't like asking.

"How much do you think?" I didn't have time for this.

I had no idea where to begin. "Please don't tell me they're anything like a hundred quid."

"The price in the book is one-eighty." I groaned. "Now, don't be like that. My contact will let us have them—"

"So you've not bought them yet?"

"Oh, no, no. He'll let us have them for …" and he couldn't stop grinning, "twenty," he mouthed. "My contact has done me an absolutely cracking deal."

It felt that a weight had been lifted from my shoulders. Twenty quid, back then, could literally be the difference between, you know, like I've already said, but twenty pounds for a piece of kit that would help prevent us being fleeced sounded like a wise investment. Then I looked at the boxes for the manufacturer's name – or, for that matter, any symbol that was recognisable. There was none.

"And do you normally make so much profit on electronics, then?" Maybe I was in the wrong game.

"I only wish I did. No, this is a one-off. And when these are gone, there's no more."

I wasn't so sure. "Have you seen one of these actually out of the box?"

"Oh, don't need to."

"We need to have one, or better still, two of them out and working to take round the shops."

"But why? I deal in electronics – look at all these boxes with amps and keyboards, tens of thousands of pounds' worth, enough to buy whatever you're worth twenty times over – more, maybe – so I know what I'm talking about, for god's sake. No, these are sound enough, take it from me."

Rita lost money. A man went in, said he wanted to buy a plate – a plate? She sold it for 50p (commercial plates cost more than that, but ... well, never mind) and he paid with a fifty pound note. She was unaware of the warnings regarding such high denomination currency, and took it, and it turned out that it was indeed genuine. But then he asked if she would change the two twenties she'd just given him for smaller notes, which she was pleased to do – after all, they had just come out of her till, hadn't they? Wrong! He'd been secreting the forged notes, I suspect, behind the plate he'd wanted to buy. We tried this in the shop, and that's the only way we could work out that the con had been done. The twenties were bad ones, not even as good as those PC Skipper had shown me. Forty quid was a biggish loss to a tiny café.

I told her that if she had a radio, such instances could be circulated around the town and the offender caught or cornered within minutes. She said she wouldn't be able to afford a radio for at least seven weeks, now that she'd lost cash, and would we be willing to hold one for her? Writing about this now, over 20 years later, £20 and £40 no longer seem such desperate amounts, but back then things were so different.

Ram-Raid Roger was holding a radio, feeling it, admiring the chunky plastic finish. "I hope you realise that opening just one of these means that now we've bought them all."

"So what do you think? Is it okay?"

"The sound quality is superb. Have a listen to this," and he switched it on, accompanied by lots of crackles and whines and whistles.

"Yeah, almost high-fidelity, isn't it?"

"Just need to find a channel, that's all..." He twiddled the knob, which was as big as a skateboard wheel, until the interference was replaced with crystal clear audio. It seemed to be a conversation between a man and a woman. "There, now what do you think to that?"

"I wonder what the range is?"

"Over a mile, so he said."

"Where's the instructions?"

"Oh, you don't need to bother with them. I mean, look, it's simple enough. Any fool could use one of these."

"I want to know what it says in the book about different frequencies."

He sighed. "Well ... the English language version hasn't arrived yet. He's ordered one for us, that we can photocopy for anyone that wants one."

"What language is the original?"

"Er ... Russian."

"I thought so. At least the range is good – bloody marvellous, in fact. Those two are in Australia."

"What? Are they? ... Yes, they certainly sound

Australian. But they can't possibly be there – that's too far."

"You're right. It's the incidental music that gives it away." He listened, then his face fell. "That's an episode of *Neighbours* we're listening to."

He held the radio at arm's length, staring at it incredulously. "How on earth is that possible?"

I had no idea; I wasn't the expert, not like he was, but now it seemed that we were back at square one.

13

Shove on the Dole

SHARON WASN'T IN THE next day, and after opening the shop the MD had gone out to look at something with his wife, leaving the apprentice to run the shop all alone, telling him it would be good experience for him. I arrived to find Greville on a stepladder, head on one side against the ceiling, peering into the video camera's viewfinder. He looked angry, yet strangely satisfied.

Then the lights dimmed, the till set up a beeping noise, the alarm siren began to wail and Greville overbalanced and fell onto the counter. The fluorescent lights flickered and I reset the alarm, then asked if he was okay. Rubbing his arm, he looked dazed, which was normal for him, so I moved on.

"There must have been one hell of a drain on the supply," I said. The last time anything like that happened was in the days when the whole shop was wired using cloth-covered lamp flex and the MD switched on the circular saw. That used to make the lights go dim, but there was a good excuse for it. So what had caused this one? "This is rather suspicious. I'd better check the upstairs rooms for smells of burning."

"Never mind about that – look at this. I think I've got one of the bandits," he spat.

He described what had happened. A man,

maybe early-40s, with a goatee beard and short ponytail, brought two items to the counter, one of which was a Stanley plane, the other a Chubb security lock. Both items were expensive, amounting to almost £50, and of a similar size.

"Hello, I wonder if you can help me, mate. It's just that I bought these from you last Saturday and I'd like to change both of them." He wanted a more expensive lock that we didn't stock, and a bigger smoothing plane.

First of all, did he have the receipts?

"Not on me, no. My wife bought them and she's got them in her bag, but she's at work. I really need to get the lock fitted this morning and I have a joiner coming specially to do it."

So Greville went to the lock display board. "Sorry, but we don't carry the one you're after, but we could order you one for tomorrow." He was most helpful.

"That's no good to me, you see, because the joiner's due at—" and he made a point of checking his watch "—half-eleven, and I really need one for then. And what about the plane? My wife bought the wrong size. That's for the door, anawl."

At this stage, Greville was wondering why the joiner didn't have his own smoothing plane, but offered to get him one for that afternoon – a pretty good service (which would mean me driving especially to the wholesaler in Bradford).

"Oh, dear, that won't do, I'm afraid. Look, I'm very sorry, but I think you'll have to give me my money back."

There was something about the wording, all

apologetic, and his tone that was like some sort of *open sesame* for the till. Greville opened it and stared into its recesses. He knew what was – or rather, *wasn't* – in there.

"There isn't enough in here," he said.

"There must be!"

He shook his head. "Apart from the bronze, fifty pences and a few pound coins, there's nothing."

"What about five pound notes and tenners?"

Greville shook his head. He almost looked embarrassed. "Sorry, can't do it. You'll have to come back later, when we've had some customers in and sold some stuff," he said, moving the plane and the lock beneath the top shelf of the counter.

"What time, do you think that'll be? Eleven o'clock? D'ya think you'll have taken enough by then?"

Greville shrugged his shoulders. "Dunno. Sometimes it's really quiet Monday morning."

"Can you let me have anything? How much d'ya have in pound coins?"

"Haven't got many. Can't spare them. Might need 'em to give in change."

"You see, it's my lad's birthday today, and I'm wanting to get him a bike..." and so it went on, but no way would our apprentice give in.

At the beginning of the recording, we saw what Greville was looking at in the camera's viewfinder: the man looked around the shop, checking for suitable items that had similar options but for which we had no stock, and ones that he could tuck into his coat. He walked down to the door, turned and pretended to come in with our stock in his hands. It was all there on tape. So was his face, clearly and for all to see.

We waited for him to show up again, as arranged, which he never did, just like the police said he wouldn't. We now had a scammer on cam, and I would quickly make a copy to show the other shops, then let the police have the original as evidence. Yes, compliments were in order for Greville, who, when facing a con artist single-handed, stood his ground, showing that not all the wisdom Sharon and I tried to impart floated right through his skull.

"I was shitting bricks," he said.

"I'm sure there's a better way of phrasing how you were feeling," I suggested. "You were exceptionally fearful of what might happen."

"That's what I've just said, shitting bricks. And there's a package, I put it on the desk. It's not addressed to anybody."

It contained copies of police mugshots, names and offences, including scams and other forms of deception such as shoplifting and a bit of opportunist burglary. I identified the CoD parcel scam woman. She was 19, looked 25, an offender since 13. This was sensitive stuff, and we would pass copies around to the other shops. Slowly, we were gaining more advantages.

Having accepted my quote, the lady with the old chest asked me to call one Monday morning to wax it for her and also to advise on her supports, as she called them, something on which she rightly assumed I was an expert. Actually, it was the iron hinges for the lid she was referring to, each one wrought by hand, gaining centuries of pitting, oxidisation and that lovely patination that only time can apply. Like a true philistine, she asked me to paint them a gaudy gold colour. I refused.

"It's my chest," she said. "By rights I can do what I like with it."

Yes she could, I told her, but she didn't have any right in making me ruin what was a valuable, historical piece. I had standards, ethical considerations; I couldn't be bought.

"I can easily get someone else to gob some paint on the dratted ugly things."

I took exception to her choice of terminology, but then she asked how much I would do it for and we agreed on a price. Well, not so much agreed as I plucked an exorbitant figure out of thin air and she said okay, and when might we get down to doing it? I looked over her shoulder, out into the muck road that ran behind the rows of terrace houses where she lived, and that's when I saw him: tall, broad-shouldered, potentially intimidating, especially if he were bearing down on you. By the time I had recognised who he was, he would be well gone.

"...so tell me when's good for you. I'm free same time tomorrow. I'd like to get it all done before my hubby gets back, be a bit of a surprise for him…"

I was out the back door before she had time to finish, down the path, cursing the latch on the gate (that I had repaired the previous week) and racing out into the hard-packed dirt road. He was out of sight, so I just ran in the same direction he'd been walking, making quick glances along the way in case he'd turned into one of the yards. When I saw him walking down Shitlingthorpe Road with a short woman, I shot through a convenient alleyway so I could pop out further down the road and face him head-on. Finger outstretched (I read it's an old stone-age thing), I approached him, then stared at the woman.

She was maybe in her mid-50s – and I mean an old mid-50s, not like the energetic career girls about town that we get today. With her hairstyle and clothes, she was like an old grandmother from the 1930s, but it was her wrinkle-free, boyish face that caught my attention.

"Shift out of my way," the man bawled, pushing against me with his sticking-out belly.

"You owe me fifty quid."

He pushed my shoulder aside. "I've no idea what you're talking about, so clear off, before I—"

"What – what will you do, huh? You conned fifty quid from my friend and I want it back."

There was bodily contact. I was managing to hold him back, but he was intent on bulldozing me out of the way. The woman looked embarrassed, and tried to calm him. He eased off, grunting, looking like he might at any second collapse. She smacked his arm and turned to me.

"It wasn't *that* much—"

"Enough to put her out of business. Just because she had a shop, it didn't mean she was wealthy."

She shook her head. "What are you going to do about it? You don't know where we live, there's nothing to stop us just walking off."

"I'd get the police. It wouldn't take them ten minutes to find you. You've been on their most wanted list for the past week."

The man stopped dying. "Don't take any notice, Barbara. The police aren't interested in us."

"Wanna bet? They've got a file this thick—" and I gestured a couple of inches, which was a bit of an exaggeration, I'll admit, "—on you and your friends."

The woman spoke. "What friends?" and she looked at him.

"All your mates that have been decimating Little Sniffingham town centre with just about every damned con-trick in the book."

"That's not us! There's only us two, and we only do it when we have to."

This was a bit of a blow to me. I didn't have a mobile phone (known as cell phones back then, after the American term), but the lady with the chest was only a few yards away and I was certain I could get a police car there within ten or fifteen minutes. Describing this pair, one called Barbara, to the inhabitants would surely provide identification. But, if they weren't part of the scammer gang...

"Go away, little lad, and play somewhere else."

"Give me the money and I'll leave you alone."

The woman was beginning to look distraught. "We don't have it. If we did, I'd give it to you, really

I would."

I stepped away, not happy. So the MD was right: these petty crims weren't part of the scammer gang. They were an unfortunate pair, with ill-fitting, charity shop clothes. I caught eye contact with her as they shuffled away down the street. The look in her eyes wasn't right. Sharon once told me that a good actor says much more with their eyes than purely with dialogue, which is why some of the old theatre artistes didn't translate too well to the cinema screen in the 1930s. I watched them for around a hundred yards down the road until they turned left. That was enough for me. Three minutes later I pulled up outside The Pig and Ferret pub.

It was a busy day, with many of the town's unemployed crowding at the bar to be served. Monday was the day they collected their dole money from the Post Office – that's merely an observation. A quick scout around and I spotted my pair just as they were about to be served.

14

Attack of the Grab Monsters

I RUSHED INTO THE SHOP to tell Sharon what had happened. She broke off from serving just long enough to warn me not to go into the office.

"The old man's in there," she said.

"So what's changed?"

"I'd leave him alone for a bit, if I was you," and she returned to her customer.

Well, telling me not to do a thing has always had the opposite effect. I found him in there, sitting at the desk, like he usually did, but instead of filling in the taxation paperwork using his trademark wide-leaded carpenter's pencil (that he'd knifed down to a nicely-rounded point, making it easier to erase mistakes), he was just sitting there, which wasn't like him at all. I asked what was wrong.

"Oh, nothing."

"Come on, something's happened – I can tell. Look at the state of you."

"You cheeky young bugger, there's nowt at all wrong wi' me ... not that... never mind." He picked up his pencil, adjusted his glasses to see the paperwork, then threw it down again. I thought it better to leave him alone for a bit.

I served customers, desperately wanting to speak with Sharon, but the door bell always sounded and another half-dozen or so would come in. Okay, so we needed the footfall, as well as the conversions to actual sales, but sometimes the irony could be mind-crippling. Eventually, it eased and I left Greville holding the fort.

"He's been done," Sharon said, taking in a deep breath. "And he's taken it bad. Thought he knew all the tricks, convinced himself that he could spot a con from across town, but this little bitch got him. I told him not to feel bad abart it – it was only a tenner, for gawd's sake, but he finks if he can drop ten quid—"

"He dropped it? I thought he'd been con—"

"Quiet, Greville! You're serving, remember." She turned back to me. "Thinks if he can lose a tenner just like that, it could be much more some other day. He's not a happy man. He ain't taking it well. And I feel sorry for him." Sharon's support for the MD was certainly a first; at any other time they wouldn't be able to stand the sight of each other, and now he had our bit-part actress-cum-full-time sales assistant in his corner, whether he liked her stuffed in there or not.

That evening, after the MD had left, we three stayed behind to watch the tape of the incident. We were watching in black and white, which made identification of the bank notes a bit awkward, but, thanks to the audio track, we could work out what had happened.

The woman, looking to be in her late-thirties, bought a cup hook costing 10p. We recognised this sale – as small as it was – as establishing her as a customer, so someone the shopkeeper – in this case the MD – would be willing to help. Yes, 10p was all that was required to, psychologically, make her an ally. But instead of leaving, she produced a £20 note and asked if he could change it for two tenners, which he did. At this point everyone was square. So far so good.

But still she didn't leave, and instead she rattled inside her handbag, swirling what sounded like a load of loose coins, and asked if she could swap ten pounds' worth for a £10 note. Now, shops are almost always short of change (as they call it), and are charged a fee at the bank for acquiring it from them, so a member of the public who wants to lighten their pocket or bag is indeed seen as a friend.

She counted the coins in her hands, then placed them on the counter, holding out her hand for the MD's £10 note, which he gave her. Still she didn't leave – which was just as well because the change was £1 short. She apologised and handed over £1. Then she offered him the £10 note he'd just given to her, saying, "You might as well give me back my twenty, then we're all square."

Did you see what happened there? The con was executed through confusion, engineering a second transaction whilst the first one was unfinished – the very same one that caught out Rita at the café.

We watched it back a couple more times, amazed at the skill on the part of the scammer, and the total ease with which it was executed. We reckoned that £100 could be ripped away per hour – more in a large town centre. Most shop workers would be unaware that anything had happened until they tried balancing the tills at the end of the day. The MD, on the other hand, instinctively felt there was something wrong and balanced as soon as she'd gone – or didn't balance, rather.

There was an upside, though: we now had another face to pass around, and a detailed description of the con trick. I was certain that no one else would fall victim to this scam, not in this town, just so long as they read the warning that PC Skipper and I sent round, with its description of the con and our advice not to enter into any offer to exchange money.

From a scammer's point of view, the means of raising the value of a note by 50% is perhaps highly-prized in terms of speed, detectability, duplication in a small area and in a small space of time, there are no parcels or packages to prepare, no voting lists to consult for names and addresses, and no telephone directories or smelly old trainers to source. It is virtually invisible, and a gang could easily fleece thousands from a large shopping centre in just one morning.

We received messages about similar attempts, all of which from then on were foiled by the shops' reluctance to participate. Then one day there was a marked absence of shop watch messages, and it was the same the day after that. It seemed as if the scammer gang, hopefully because of the scam details we had shared, had moved on to pastures new. We could only hope, for the sake of other traders, that they were able to contain the losses as we had in Little Sniffingham. But the scammers had one last attack, as a kind of farewell, bless them.

I was negotiating with a woman about how much I would charge to replace a tubular mortice latch in one of her doors. She told me that her husband could do it cheaper, so I asked her why she was asking me for a price. And she said it was because she'd thought that her husband was too expensive – now work that one out. Anyhow, a large van pulled up outside, which I thought was a bit strange as we weren't expecting a delivery. The door jangler sounded. And that's when it happened.

The lights were switched off. A woman screamed. Another one joined in. Men roared like lions, and suddenly we were overrun with small children running around, also screaming, pushing stock off the shelves. We still had the illuminated Black & Decker display stand, where I caught a glimpse of a man ripping out the 2-foot tubes and casting them to the floor before scooping the power tool accessories into a giant bag. Elsewhere, the other man and the two women were doing the same, screaming, indiscriminately grabbing anything that was loose, whilst the children laughed and screamed and ran amok.

Thrown into the dark and confusion, never having experienced nor heard of anything like this before, we were powerless (no pun intended). I chased, tried grabbing the adult assailants, only to be beaten about the legs and groin by spanner-bearing part-sized demons, cackling like toothless witches in a school play.

The shop's ground floor was basically two large rooms, and the adults and children streamed into both, leaving no area untouched – tools, batteries, with an unerring instinct for spotting high-ticket items that were grabbed and bagged. I recognised the young woman who'd done the CoD scam and I tried grabbing hold of her arm, but missed. I remember the look on her face: it was not pleasant, a career criminal if ever I saw one. And throughout was the jarring cacophony that made my teeth tingle.

There was a further round of muffled banging and shrieking. I shot into the main shop in time to see the lot of them pile into the van. Running back into the other room I watched through the large display window as it sped away. It was then the cellar trapdoor opened. Thinking that one of them had hidden down there, I was ready to slam it closed and weight it down until the police came; I just wanted to see which one it was, hoping it wasn't one of the kids. Then I thought, *Don't be stupid – a child wouldn't be strong enough to open that...*

I recognised the face staring up at me: short, dark hair and pointy noise, only this time her expression was one of apprehension.

"What's going on? Is there a fire?"

I told her not to worry and to take care of all the

broken glass on the floor when she came out.

The attack had lasted just over one minute. My lady customer's bag had been grabbed, the other customers had cowered under the stairs, having followed Greville in there. It must have been a tight and intimate fit, as I knew from experience (don't ask; that's another story). The MD came out of the office, adjusting his hearing aid and demanding to know what all the noise was about. Sharon had been frisked, and she stepped out into the aisle, wondering how to deal with the shock of it all. Her hair was a mess, so was mine (yes, back then I did). We decided that we didn't suffer shock, so switched the main lights back on, called the police and comforted our customers, once we'd found them all. The glue girl took a brush and shovel and made a start on cleaning up the mess. There was plenty of it.

15

Cold Light of Day

I NEVER FOUND OUT why, instead of going home, the glue girl had preferred to stay in our cellar: cold, damp, with the shuffles of all the spirits of those who had lived and worked in that building over the past couple of centuries. She had an ancient single-bar electric heater that she'd rescued from a waste skip, which explained why the lights went dim. And it must have felt to be a million miles away from where she really belonged.

But then, at some point, maybe we all need to experience something that helps us to appreciate what we've had all along, like someone to care for us. Or maybe someone for us to care for.

I asked if the money she'd left had been for glue. No, she'd taken candles and a gas canister for a camping stove she had with her, and promised to pay what she still owed because she didn't want to be a criminal. I told her that it wouldn't be necessary, and I got the MD to run her home.

The police didn't turn up until the next day because they were dealing with victims of the town centre attack in alphabetical order. Being L, we were some way down the list. There was the video footage, of course, which is when we found that Greville's camera used an old system that didn't see at all well in dark conditions, so all we had was the noise and a lot of blurred movement.

The children, though, I did recognise: they were the same ones begging outside the Abbey National. Read into that what you will.

After this one last comment on their ability to get away with taking what belongs to other people, the scammer gang never again troubled Little Sniffingham, nor did we ever learn where they moved next, nor whatever became of them.

"There's someone in the shop!" The MD said, spilling his tea. Greville and I looked at each other, by which time Sharon was already out there, scanning the aisles, the nooks and the crannies. This happened frequently, and sometimes the footstep was so definite that we would even check the cellar. We never found anyone there.

"Bleeding hell, Graham, it's cold enough to freeze my tits off," said Maggie, rubbing her arms and wearing those unattractive gloves with the missing fingers. "Where the hell have you been? I've been waiting ages for you coming with that."

With resignation, I sighed. "Shall I take it straight through for you?"

"Yes, love, and mind your shins on that bloody shelf. I'll have to get that sorted, when I've a minute. I say, Graham, d'ya fancy some coffee? ... Thought you might. I got the pots ready, just in case. Just go through, I'll be with you in a minute."

THE END

SOME SELF-PORTRAITS

Bonus Chapter

Stepping back in time ... an independent remembers

From *DIY Week*, October 2016

In 1979, as an ex- bank cashier turned shop assistant, with increased hours and reduced pay. It felt the only prospects I had were of sliding into terminal poverty. With pretty much non-existent practical skills, I was to DIY what a toothpick was to deep-core mining.

Slab attack

The boss was an ex-Royal Navy man, where he'd served as a joiner. It seemed that every job he'd done on board was during some sort of attack – either from the enemy or the elements. Storms, sinkings and wreckage were all in a day's work and to hear him talk you'd think he'd spent more time at sea than Davy Jones.

"We're under attack!" he said one day, looking into the street. The council was lifting the old Victorian paving flags and replacing them with shiny black tarmac. Lovely. We later found that old flags were attracting premium prices as architectural antiques, and the council philistines were making a killing on them. Suddenly the boss shot outside to have words with the driver of the power roller that had just crunched our Edwardian coal grate. I wondered who'd be paying for its replacement if, indeed, there were any still available. Three days later we were fortunate enough to be presented with a concrete slab to block up the hole. It was lucky that no one had fallen down there.

Lady's friend

Unkind locals warned me about daft Doris, an aged lady who scurried around town in her pre-war coat and hat. She could be seen on the streets poking around in corners, shop doorways and litter bins. I asked the boss what she was looking for. "The 1930s," he grunted.

The first time I served her, I was failing to explain about her suspect ballcock washer when suddenly she began talking to another person – only I couldn't see them. Bluetooth hadn't been invented, remember. Assuming it was a mental health issue, maybe I should join in to make her feel better? But that wouldn't work as I didn't know what this other person was saying – hang on a sec, did I really believe there was some invisible presence witnessing my pathetic sales technique? After a few stern words, Doris told them to shut up and we got back to the workings of her toilet. Such was life.

Size matters

If I told you how small was the shop, you'd wonder

how the boss ever managed to pay me anything more than a paper-round wage (which was how it felt), but every day there were times when 10 or more people would cram in there, eager to buy what they thought could make their homes that little bit more complete and their lives happier. The DIY superstores hadn't quite reached where we were in the back of beyond, but it was clear that things were screaming out for change. We had just 215 square feet in which to trade, and when I saw it empty a few years ago it felt about as big as a telephone box. How on earth did we manage? All we had was the shop and a room next door where we cut wood to size and the boss parked his car.

Many of the town's shops had been face-lifted, having had the traditional covered doorways torn out and replaced with the new bog-standard flat-frontages. Okay, so this modernisation increased internal floor space, but it also zapped people being able to look in the display windows as they sheltered from the rain. Yes, maybe it was an old-fashioned design but, just like the water culverts installed by the Victorians – who really knew how to control drainage – it was design for purpose. But such ideas are easy to discard just because some modern-day bright sparks think they know better.

It was obvious that to survive in a changing marketplace we should follow our fellow traders by going down the self-service route, and there was only one direction we could expand and I knew it wouldn't go down well with the boss. "It's a bloody tale!" he said. "We're not doing that. What about the car?" I mentioned the car parks, every one of them free (oh, happy days!). We'd change the double doors for a huge display window and make a walk-round store like other shops. "I don't give a damn what everyone else is doing," was his response. Yep, this was going to take some time, and I would need to develop a strategy for convincing him that progress was essential.

Purr-fect ending

"Where is it?" Doris screeched. It appeared she'd come in just to have a conversation, but not with me. I wanted to get back to sorting out piles of wood offcuts into cheap bundles for the hobbyists and firewood customers – the first stage in my expansion plan.

"Tell me again," she said, getting agitated with her friend. "I can't hear you!" Then she looked straight at me. "You've got a cat." I denied it. "No, but you have. It's a baby kitten and it's in your cellar. It'll die if you don't get it out," and she left.

Opening the trapdoor would mean humping the recent stock delivery out of the way, but something about her tone made me shift all the boxes and go down there. I emerged holding a tiny, tortoiseshell moggy, cold and shivering – which made two of us, but for different reasons.

Before you go ...

Thank you so much for reading
this book. I hope you enjoyed it.
If you did, I would really appreciate
you leaving a few kind words as a review
on Amazon UK or Amazon US.

Maybe you can also recommend it to friends,
readers' groups and discussion boards,
which would be great. Thank you.

Visit me at grahamhigson.com
and click **Keep me updated**

Also by Graham Higson

The first story with Sharon, Greville and the gang...

You can buy anything in the local hardware shop – well almost. It's the legendary Aladdin's cave with fixes for everything from a leaking pipe, a shattered groyne, a wobbly bladder (should that be ladder?) to a broken heart. And some remedies are not so easy to find...

This semi-autobiographical and humorous work by Yorkshire writer Graham Higson looks back to the end of an era for that almost extinct of species, the local hardware shop.

Peopled with a variety of oddball, but mainly

gentle, characters, Graham takes us back to his 1990s' world with the struggles of an essential component of the British high street in its attempts to compete with the multiples, whilst also coping with the fall-out from the decline of trustworthy, customer-driven banking and a variety of sharp business practices.

There are multiple layers to this book and it reflects so many aspects of our changing society ... An intriguing and fascinating book which you cannot fail to enjoy.
Robert Fear, author

This book is one man's memoir—a treasure trove of anecdotes, some tinged with humour, others with disappointment, some are downright bizarre—his guide to observing life from behind a shop counter.

I very much enjoyed the conversational style and the strong down to earth Yorkshire voice ... It gave the anecdotes such realism and humour.
Rebecca Hislop, reader

Humour so visual and the gags just keep a-coming ... as cheeky as its title! ... At the end of this book I was smiling from ear to ear.
Frank Kusy, author

About the author

GRAHAM HIGSON lives in an outlying Pennine village and shares this blustery environment with a growing collection of books, his understanding wife and a workshop piled high with offcuts of oak. His two grown-up children are among his best friends.

He has a BSc degree in technology (in which he managed to sneak a course about playwriting), and an MA in Professional Writing. Having written professionally for over 25 years (and then some, he says), ***Oak Seer: A Supernatural Mystery*** was the first of his published novels, followed by **Flither Lass,** a historical novel set during the First World War. His fictionalized memoir ***How Much for a Little Screw?*** was based on his years working as a hardware man.

His hobbies include art, swimming, reading, watching lots of screen drama, helping to republish the novels of Leo Walmsley, and searching for that elusive moment of self-discovery – though there's no sign of it yet, he says.

www.grahamhigson.com

Printed in Poland
by Amazon Fulfillment
Poland Sp. z o.o., Wrocław